CHARLES PALMER

More Than Just A Gentleman

CHARLES PALMER

More Than Just A Gentleman

Douglas Miller

FAIRFIELD BOOKS

Fairfield Books
17 George's Road, Fairfield Park, Bath BA1 6EY
Tel 01225-335813

First published 2005

ISBN 0 9544886 1 X

Printed and bound in Great Britain by
Bath Press Ltd, Bath

For Barbara
in fond memory of Charles

CHARLES HENRY PALMER

Born 15 May 1919

Died 31 March 2005

CONTENTS

ABOUT THIS BOOK

Charles Palmer had been wanting to co-operate in the writing of a book for some years. His motive for such a venture was not any personal glory. Rather, he had enjoyed a most pleasurable life in cricket, and he wanted to share memories of that pleasure with others.

With typical modesty he was uncertain that anybody would want to read such a book, but he was persuaded to set to work by Sylvia Michael, dedicated archivist at Leicestershire County Cricket Club, and Davinder Sandhu, a personal friend. The intention was that Davinder would visit him regularly, go through all his memorabilia and set down on paper his stories.

By Autumn 2004 some early chapters had been written, and Charles sent them to me, wondering whether I thought that they would be of any interest to anybody. He also expressed concern that he was 85 years of age and that, with Davinder a busy hospital consultant, the project was not moving fast enough.

So in October we all met at his golf club, and it was arranged that Douglas Miller would take over the task of writing the book, with Fairfield Books agreeing to publish the result. Douglas had just completed a book with the Glamorgan cricketer Don Shepherd, and he had the time to put in some long hours of intensive work. Davinder was delighted to know that the project was moving forward, and Sylvia offered every support.

Douglas worked tirelessly, meeting up with Charles on several occasions and visiting many of his friends and colleagues, right back to his days as a schoolmaster in Bromsgrove in the 1940s. He and I talked regularly, and the plan was to have the book in print by August 2005.

Alas, in the months from Christmas to Easter, Charles' health went into serious decline, and his meetings with Douglas became less frequent. Douglas continued with his other interviews, hoping to fill in gaps with Charles at a later point, but it was not to be. On Good Friday Charles was admitted to hospital, and he died the following Thursday, 31st March.

The book stood incomplete, but such was the progress that Douglas had already made that we all decided that it would be best if we went ahead with what we had. In this respect it proved a bonus that I had twice interviewed Charles for magazine articles, and the book's account of his tour of the West Indies contains a great deal from these conversations.

Much of this text was written while Charles was alive. 'Charles recalls,' it says, or 'Charles thinks'. We have decided to leave it like that.

Charles was a gentleman but, as the title says, he was much more than that. He was a fine cricketer, a much-respected administrator, and he was a pleasure to know. Whatever the difficulties he faced, he never forgot that cricket was a game, played for fun and for friendship.

It was his wish that this book would give pleasure, and we offer it as a tribute to him in the hope that we have fulfilled that wish.

Stephen Chalke Fairfield Books

AUTHOR'S INTRODUCTION

I first met Charles Palmer in October 2004. Immediately I was captivated by his charm, his wit and his boundless sense of fun.

As I talked to those who had played under Charles' captaincy at Leicester, I grew to expect one word to describe their former skipper. Above all else, they would tell me, Charles was a 'gentleman'.

But beneath the urbane and friendly exterior lay so much more. Good manners and charm alone could not have lifted Leicestershire from the wooden spoon to the upper places in the Championship in the 1950s. And it took more than old-fashioned courtesy to restore the county's precarious balance sheet. On the field and in committee there was a steely sense of purpose: 'Charles Palmer: more than just a gentleman.'

Charles took office as President of MCC shortly after the election of Pope John Paul II, and he opened his first meeting by telling the committee that they now had in the chair a man who was older than the Pope. With his enthusiastic co-operation in the writing of this book, it never seemed possible that Charles would fail to outlive the pontiff, whose health had long given concern in Rome. Yet, by a matter of days, it was Charles who died first, at the end of March 2005. Sadly he had failed to see the book through to completion.

As I shared the early drafts of chapters with him, Charles would offer nothing but encouragement. "I must save up to buy this book," was his favourite quip.

By the time of Charles' death most of our essential conversations had taken place, but there were still questions I wanted to ask. His passing also brought an increased responsibility to complete the book in the manner he would have wished. Cricket was a game he had loved and respected, and his wish was to share the pleasure it had brought him – with a few chuckles along the way.

From his early years with Leicestershire, Charles was in demand as a speaker. His files carry a repertoire of witty stories that helped him on his way, and he always liked to leave his audience with an uplifting message which he especially urged me to include in this book.

"It is so important to maintain high standards and to uphold the decencies, dignities and courtesies which have characterised cricket ever since I entered the game."

Douglas Miller
June 2005

9

CHAPTER 1

THE INNINGS OF A LIFETIME

Wednesday 28th April 1948. A new cricket season was getting under way with the visit of the Australians to New Road, Worcester. With six summers lost to war, this was the first Australian side to tour England for ten years, and their captain Don Bradman named his strongest eleven for this opening match. A spring heat wave had given way to slate grey skies and a chill wind, with squally showers in the offing, but neither the weather nor a mid-week start could dampen the anticipation. By dawn a queue had begun to form outside the gates of the New Road ground, and at 9.30 it was snaking back across the Severn Bridge.

There was hope in the air, as there always is with cricket. Hope that England would regain the Ashes after their disastrous tour of Australia eighteen months earlier. Hope that the golden summer of 1947 would return and that Compton and Edrich would make runs as they had against the South Africans. Hope that somewhere new talent would be unearthed and that, under English skies, Bradman's all-conquering Australians could be vanquished. And in Worcester there was hope that the county, traditionally first to play the tourists, could strike first blood as they had done against the Indians and South Africans in the previous two years.

With the boundary rope brought in to accommodate more spectators on the grass, the gates closed with nearly 15,000 huddled inside the ground, all of them wrapped up against the elements. No other first-class matches would start until the weekend so all the nation's leading cricket correspondents had descended upon Worcester, their frozen fingers poised over their typewriters as the two captains went out to toss. On his three previous visits to the ground Bradman had scored 236, 206 and 258, but Worcestershire captain Allan White won the toss and his decision to bat meant that the correspondents would first have to pass judgment on Ray Lindwall and Keith Miller, the world's best opening attack, now operating in harness.

'Flags and bunting writhed in a high wind, which seemed at first to carry a chill of disappointment,' reported the *Evening Despatch*. The second ball of the match, bowled by Lindwall, swung into the young Don Kenyon's pads and 'umpire Root promptly answered Lindwall's lone appeal.'

Worcestershire had lost their first wicket without a run on the board and, as the disconsolate Kenyon returned to the pavilion, a slightly built figure emerged through the gate to replace him.

Charles Palmer. Those in possession of the *News Chronicle*'s pocket-sized Cricket Annual, price one shilling, could look up his details:

> **C.H. PALMER** – Sound Batsman. First played for the county in 1938 and in following season scored 993 runs, including three centuries. Headed Worcester averages last year with 616 (average 44) in 15 innings. Is a

master at Bromsgrove School and available only during vacation. Born Old Hill, May 15, 1919.

Charles still vividly remembers that walk to the middle to face Lindwall. "I had been told by so many people what a devastating away swinger he could bowl at speed, and all the way from the pavilion to the wicket I kept on saying 'Don't follow his away swinger, don't follow his away swinger, don't follow his away swinger.'"

He took guard, looked round the field and prepared for the dreaded outswinger. Lindwall's first ball to the new batsman was a surprise, an attempted yorker, but it was over-pitched and Charles met it on the full toss, whipping it backward of square leg to the boundary. He was off the mark, and by the end of the over he had added a second boundary, though this time 'Palmer knew little about it as his snick went off the wicket-keeper's glove to the rails.' "Yes, that was a superb away swinger which I did follow. I was lucky to get away with it."

The young schoolmaster was soon into his stride, 'driving and hooking with ease and power'. While his experienced partner Eddie Cooper was resolute in defence, Charles Palmer took the attack to the Australians. An on drive for four and a pull for six off Toshack took him to 50 in as many minutes and, when he straight drove Miller to the boundary to raise the partnership's hundred, his share was 74. According to *Wisden*, 'his driving was glorious.'

Etched clearly in Charles' mind is a brief duel with Keith Miller. "I had pushed Miller through the covers for four runs. It ran very fast down that part of the ground at Worcester, even though it was wet. And, as I recall, Miller used to advertise that he was going to bowl a bouncer because his mane went up and down, didn't it? And I thought, 'This has got to be a bouncer after a four like that.' So I did a bit of guesswork and went onto my back foot, hoping that it would be a bouncer, and it was." The scorebook records the two consecutive fours, though Charles has always remembered it differently. "I thought I'd hit it for six, but it must have been Toshack I hit for six!"

Rain brought the players in for an early lunch, but Charles resumed with a delightful glance to the fine leg boundary. Then, with 85 to his name, including 13 fours and one six, and the scoreboard showing a total of 137 for one, 'he swung carelessly across Toshack's good-length ball and was caught by Johnson at midwicket.' In the view of the *Manchester Guardian*, it was 'his only bad shot'.

Cooper's patient knock soon came to an end, and there was little more than a few brave blows from Dick Howorth before the Worcestershire innings subsided to a disappointing 233 all out. In reply there were centuries from Arthur Morris and Bradman, though the Don's 107 was something of a failure after his previous efforts on the ground. He was approaching his 40th birthday, and Charles remembers speaking to him as he left the wicket: "I said to him when he was out, 'You're slipping, you only got a hundred.' He said, 'I gave it away. I'm tired.'"

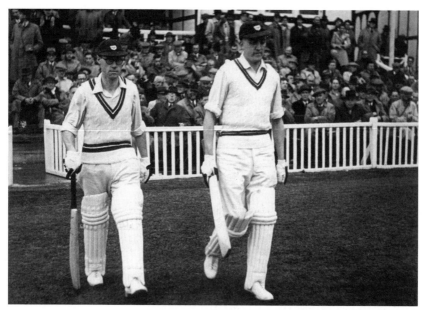

Charles Palmer and Eddie Cooper, going back out after lunch on the first day

On the final day Worcestershire batted again 229 behind and, though they lost by an innings and 17 runs, Charles further enhanced his reputation, making light of an injury sustained in the field with 'a well-composed 34' before using his feet once too often to be stumped off McCool.

EW Swanton in the *Daily Telegraph* noted that Palmer's runs had been made 'as easefully as FE Woolley might have done in the same circumstances a dozen years ago. His method looked sound all through with quickness of footwork, sound judgment of the ball's length and a beautiful pair of wrists.' 'He is about Bradman's build,' wrote Alex Bannister in the *Daily Mail*, 'and has the footwork and timing which bear the stamp of class.'

The Times joined in the paeans of praise after Charles' second innings: 'Palmer again used his feet to get to the pitch of the ball, and there were some heads wagged as if to pronounce that this Australian bowling was not all it had been feared to be.'

To those reporting for the popular press it added to the charm that such fine batting should have come not from one of the county's established professionals, but from a part-timer who looked so little like a sportsman. For all his similarity of build to Bradman, reports preferred to describe the man of the hour as 'slight' and 'bespectacled' and to make playful references to his profession as a schoolmaster. 'Australians get caning from a teacher,' quipped the *Daily Mirror*, while a cartoonist celebrated by depicting the new hero in a mortarboard with the Australian captain sitting at a school desk in front of him.

Nor did reporters miss the human angle: many of Charles' pupils from Bromsgrove School had been on the ground to watch their hero's innings.

Soon their English teacher would be back in the classroom, and it seemed that he would be lost to the first-class game until late July.

As the summer wore on, and the Australians recorded victory after victory, 17 of them by an innings, it became clear that the Worcestershire amateur had, in the words of *Wisden*, 'played one of the best innings of the season against the touring side.' He may not have realised it at the time, but after his batting in this match Charles Palmer's life would never be quite the same again. "That was the pivotal point in my playing career," he now reflects. "What started with my being just a Worcestershire and locally known player was the publicity that came from that particular innings. That innings put me on a wider map, bearing in mind that I wasn't in the class of Edrich and Compton and so forth."

Among those braving the cold at Worcester was Walter Robins. With AJ Holmes and JC Clay he was one of the selectors appointed to choose the Test teams that summer. What Robins had seen made a profound impression and, while Charles retreated from the limelight to resume coaching the boys at Bromsgrove and finding time to play a few weekend matches for Old Hill in the Birmingham League, Robins was enthusing his colleagues to take note of the Worcestershire amateur's talents.

When the teams were selected for the Test trial at Edgbaston on 2nd June, Charles had only played one first-class match that summer but his 85 was still the highest score made against the tourists. So it was no surprise that he was invited to play for the Rest against England in the trial.

Such was the state of English cricket in its third summer after the war that, of the 22 players initially selected for this Test trial, the youngest at 27 years of age were Godfrey Evans and Vince Broderick, with Alec Bedser and Charles at 29 the only others below 30. The captain of the Rest side was the 37-year-old Freddie Brown, who had just played his first championship match since 1939 and, when he pulled out with an injury, he was replaced by the 42-year-old Walter Robins. In such company, Charles represented youth, with Jack Hobbs one who had pressed for his inclusion: 'A player I should like to see again is CH Palmer, the Worcestershire amateur, a fine all-round cricketer. Surely he could be spared from school in England's time of need.'

"The school was very good from that point of view," says Charles, remembering his headmaster's response to the selectors' various requests. It certainly helped that the Chairman of the Governors, Lord Cobham, was the father of Charles Lyttelton, who had been captain of Worcestershire when Charles had first played for the county before the war. "He was President of Worcestershire – and president of everything else – and I think they backed the idea. Here's a local boy, let's give him what encouragement we can."

In a Test trial spoiled by inclement weather Charles, batting at number four, managed just 11 before being bowled by Alec Bedser as the Rest struggled to 158 for nine, but he made his mark with the ball, capturing the wicket of Bill Edrich at a cost of 35 runs in 17 tidy overs. 'Palmer impressed with his good length, accurate medium-paced bowling, which the pick of England's batsmen never really mastered,' wrote Charles Harrold in the *Birmingham Gazette*.

The Rest team versus England, Edgbaston, June 1948

Standing (left to right): Charles Palmer, Harold Butler, Vince Broderick, Reg Simpson, Ken Cranston, George Emmett
Sitting: Billy Griffith, Laurie Fishlock, Walter Robins, Arthur Fagg, Bill Copson

Though not summoned to the England side that summer, Charles remained in the selectors' minds and his next release from Bromsgrove School came when he was asked to take part in the Gentlemen and Players match at Lord's in mid-July. He was at the wicket long enough for *The Times* correspondent to regard him as 'a nice batsman, altogether enjoyable to watch' before he was late to a ball on his off stump from the Warwickshire pace bowler Tom Pritchard. There were only five runs to his name and a second innings duck, bowled once again by Pritchard, meant that Charles left Lord's without enhancing his reputation.

There were a few useful innings for Worcestershire, the highest 89 against Leicestershire, but his 85 in the chill April wind remained Charles' passport to possible international honours. As early as 7th July, having at that stage played only two first-class matches in the summer, he received from MCC the first formal intimation that he might find a place in the winter touring party:

Dear Sir

I am writing to let you know that the MCC are now giving preliminary consideration to selection of a team to tour South Africa in 1948/49. The team will leave about October 7th and return about April 30th.

The selection committee are anxious to include a reasonable portion of amateur cricketers. It would be very helpful if you could say whether you could accept an invitation or not if offered later.

You will appreciate that we are approaching several other cricketers on these lines and no serious consideration will be given to the selection of the team until we have received all the players' replies.

I should be grateful therefore if you would regard this letter as confidential, though of course you are at liberty to show it to your employer.

Yours faithfully,

RS Aird

Assistant Secretary

In mid-August, when the first 14 of a 16 strong party were announced, the part-time cricketer found his name among those selected to tour South Africa that winter. One who had no doubts about his right to be in the party was Sir Donald Bradman. In his *'Farewell to Cricket'*, published in 1950, he wrote in reference to the innings at Worcester:

Charlie Palmer batted so well that he threatened at one stage to get 100 before lunch. At that time I had no idea how highly he was regarded. How close he must have been to selection in the Test matches was shown when, at the end of the season, he was invited to tour South Africa with the MCC team.

There were some good knocks played against us at various times, but apart from the batsmen who played in the Tests, none better than this splendid exhibition of stroke play by the diminutive schoolmaster.

WORCESTERSHIRE v AUSTRALIANS

Worcester, 28, 29 & 30 April 1948

AUSTRALIANS WON BY AN INNINGS & 17 RUNS

WORCESTERSHIRE

D. Kenyon	lbw b Lindwall	0	c Tallon b McCool	17
E. Cooper	c Hassett b Toshack	51	lbw b Toshack	22
C.H. Palmer	c Johnson b Toshack	85	st Tallon b McCool	34
R.E.S. Wyatt	st Tallon b McCool	18	*absent hurt*	0
L. Outschoorn	b Lindwall	1	c Tallon b Barnes	54
A.F.T. White *	c Tallon b Miller	1	c Barnes b McCool	11
R. Jenkins	b Johnson	7	lbw b Johnson	21
R. Howorth	*not out*	37	lbw b McCool	0
R.T.D. Perks	c Toshack b McCool	0	c Barnes b Johnson	27
H. Yarnold +	c Barnes b Johnson	15	c Lindwall b Johnson	11
P.F. Jackson	c Barnes b Johnson	1	*not out*	9
Extras	*b 7, lb 10*	17	*b 4, lb 1, w 1*	6
		233		**212**

1-0, 2-137, 3-158, 4-159, 5-164, 6-178, 7-178, 8-178, 9-219, 10-233
1-41, 2-41, 3-108, 4-108, 5-122, 6-165, 7-165, 8-195, 9-212

Lindwall	15	2	41	2		3	0	19	0
Miller	12	1	36	1		8	3	18	0
McCool	19	9	38	2		17	5	29	4
Toshack	14	3	39	2		18	8	40	1
Johnson	23	8	52	3		13.3	1	75	3
Barnes	9	6	10	0		8	2	25	1

AUSTRALIANS

S.G. Barnes	lbw b Howorth	44
A.R. Morris	c Jenkins b Jackson	108
D.G. Bradman *	b Jackson	107
R.R. Lindwall	lbw b Jackson	32
C.L. McCool	b Jackson	0
D. Tallon +	b Jackson	4
A.L. Hassett	c Wyatt b Jackson	35
W.A. Brown	st Yarnold b Howorth	25
K.R. Miller	*not out*	50
I. W. Johnson	*not out*	12
E.R.H. Toshack		
Extras	*b 6, lb 5, w 4*	15
	(for 8 wickets, declared) 462	

1-79, 2-265, 3-297, 4-314, 5-320, 6-335, 7-388, 8-402

Perks	26	3	95	0
Palmer	16	5	56	0
Wyatt	1	0	4	0
Jenkins	7	0	47	0
Jackson	39	4	135	6
Howorth	38	6	109	2
Outschoorn	1	0	1	0

Umpires: F. Root and D. Davies

CHAPTER 2

FROM OLD HILL TO COUNTY CRICKET

"I was very tiny – three, four or five, something like that – when my mother made me a bat out of a butter pat and bowled underarm to me in the garden."

Charles Henry Palmer was born at Old Hill in the Black Country on 15th May 1919, the only child of Clarence Wesley Palmer and Clara Nellie, formerly Homer. Both the Palmers and the Homers were long-standing Staffordshire families. Charles' father was also known as Charles after he had abandoned the name Clarence to avoid being addressed as Clarrie. The change was prompted in part by a fear of being called a sissy in the Army, but there was another difficulty: Clara was also called Clarrie. "So," as Charles points out, "there was confusion because people never knew who they were talking about, because man and wife were called the same thing."

Charles' father worked on the sales side for a builder's merchants in Blackheath, a couple of miles from Old Hill. It was his job to find customers for the company's wares, a principal line in the 1930s being grates for coal fires.

Cricket was in the blood on both sides of the family, and Charles' father and his mother's brother were both prominent members of Old Hill Cricket Club, which competed in the Birmingham League and whose ground was less than half a mile from Charles' home at 9 The Crescent. Charles senior was a fine batsman and off-spin bowler for Old Hill, while HW Homer, 'Uncle Bert', was an even better player, who opened the batting for Staffordshire and captained them in the 1930s. Bert Homer also played four times for the Minor Counties representative eleven, scoring 71 against the New Zealanders in 1931.

Both Charles' father and his uncle Bert had the same second name, Wesley. This reflected a strong strand of primitive Methodism in the family, part of a powerful non-conformist tradition in the West Midlands. "My father's uncle was a real evangelical, tub-thumping, pulpit-bashing man. If he came on a Sunday, it really was a gruesome business. You couldn't read a newspaper; you weren't allowed to play with a ball."

And what of Charles' father, was he of this persuasion? "My father was very much not of this persuasion," Charles says emphatically.

He remembers him with obvious warmth and affection. "There wasn't an ounce of malice in the old boy. He wouldn't set the world on fire but he made himself what he was, and I had tremendous respect for him for doing that."

Cricket talk reverberated around the home. "Of course my uncle was very keen, my mother was keen and my old man was, so I was brought up in a cricket loving atmosphere." But it is music that dominates Charles' early recollections. "My father became a very accomplished pianist; he taught himself. He became a very good organist as well, although he did have lessons on the organ. He enjoyed himself in things like choral works, and he used to be the choir co-ordinator. And my mother was a very good singer, a choir lady and all the rest of it: choral works and a little bit of solo work."

Charles' file of old newspaper cuttings contains a 1931 review of an amateur production of the Edwardian musical, 'The Quaker Girl', in which Mr C.W. Palmer is said to have sung 'with great acceptance throughout' while Mrs Clarrie Palmer, in the part of a maid, 'sang and acted with delicious abandon.'

The man who would later walk out to face Lindwall and Miller confesses: "I was never more terrified than when I had to accompany my mother in public when she sang some of the Elgar sea songs. I was in my middle teens, and I was far from an accomplished pianist. But I did enjoy it. I've always enjoyed playing the piano."

Charles' father at the piano

Charles carries earlier memories of keeping his father company on his musical missions. Charles senior regularly played the organ at the local Baptist church, where the young Charles, then seven or eight, would sit alongside him on the organ seat. "When there was nothing going on I'd pull the stops out, or occasionally he'd tell me what stop to pull out. But his attention to the sermon only existed if it was a damned good sermon, and there were a hell of a lot of bad ones. So sometimes you would find that the old boy had lost interest and he'd have his head in his hands and his arms on the keyboard, having a little snooze. But I knew that my cue was when the old parson said, 'And now to God the Father …' Then it was my job to switch the electric motor on for the organ. There was one lovely occasion when I'd fiddled around with the stops and I'd pulled the whole damn lot out. And, of course, immediately I pressed the motor, you can imagine the cacophony that came through! I've never seen a chap wake up so quickly in my life."

Charles began his education at the local school, a short walk from his Old Hill home, before winning a scholarship at the age of eleven to Halesowen Grammar School. Here he developed a love of Latin and English, relishing the sound of the languages and performing creditably in School Certificate. "It was a very civilised school," he recalls, "a very good school. It had a very good headmaster and very good staff, and if you've got that you've got a school, haven't you?"

It was at Halesowen School that Charles first met his future wife Barbara. She was the youngest of nine children, and her oldest sister, twenty-four years her senior, had been at school with Charles' mother. Her father, Albert Thomas Butler, was a successful architect and he, too, was a cricketer, captaining Halesowen Cricket Club.

Though Charles denies that there was any hint of romance in their school days, he does recall that he made extravagant use of his father's telephone to ring her. He would place the phone on top of the grand piano as he picked out the popular tunes of the day while Barbara, at the other end, would alert her brothers and sisters to the free concert. "And before long," says Charles, "I was playing to half the family, which was all right up to a point until the old man started shouting 'When can I use my bloody telephone?'"

Old Hill Cricket Club was a powerful force in the strong Birmingham League, and in 1932 their young leg-spinner Eric Hollies graduated from the club's first eleven to the Warwickshire side. Charles' father and uncle were first team players, and by the following summer the 14 year-old Charles Palmer was proving his worth in the second eleven, taking eight for 37 with his off-breaks. "I seem to remember that I got a hat-trick that day," he says. "And I was playing with Eric Hollies' father, Bill Hollies, who bowled underarm and got a lot of wickets."

A legendary figure in Staffordshire cricket in those years was the great Sydney Barnes. In 1928, when he was 55 years old, he was said by the West Indian tourists to have been the best bowler they encountered that summer. Charles was playing for Old Hill against Bridgnorth in July 1941 when he faced him, and already that summer the 68-year-old Barnes had taken 60 wickets.

Charles recalls a story told by his Uncle Bert, who often captained Barnes for Staffordshire: "There was a match where the interest had gone from it and he said to Barnes, 'Sydney, I reckon that, if you wanted to, you could bowl an over and nominate where the batsman would hit you.' And Sydney said, 'I reckon I could.' Apparently four out of the six balls went straight to the nominated fielder."

As soon as Charles' name began to hit the local headlines, his mother started to paste the cuttings into a maroon scrapbook, and seventy years on Charles recovers them from the depths of an oak chest. "This is all me," he announces a little sheepishly.

Correctly predicting that Eric Hollies would soon be playing for England, an early local report continues: 'They now have another lad who promises to become a brilliant all-rounder. He is 15-year-old Charlie Palmer, son of CW Palmer, a member of Old Hill's first team. This boy, who is still at Halesowen Grammar School, was recently brought into the second team and has shown remarkable all-round form.'

At Halesowen Charles was soon revealing a talent far beyond his years. For six consecutive seasons he headed the batting averages and left the school with seven centuries to his name. A highlight was 156 not out against King

Old Hill Cricket Club

Charles Palmer is seated, far right
Also seated: (third from left) Uncle Bert Homer, (centre) Billy Edwards the President

Charles Grammar School, Kidderminster, a knock that took just two hours, with the last 80 runs coming in 20 minutes.

The *News Chronicle* made nationwide weekly awards of Jack Hobbs bats for outstanding performances in club and school cricket., and the scrapbook records that he was three times listed as a candidate, once winning a bat with the great man's signature on it. Two of his listings were for school centuries, the third for an unbeaten 113 for Old Hill against Walsall.

As his school career drew to a close, a local paper was able to report that 'Charlie Palmer, who occasionally turns out for Old Hill first team in Birmingham League cricket, is being carefully watched by Worcestershire. During the Whitsun holidays he was included in the County Colts side and gave a sparkling display hitting up a not out century. It was the second time that Palmer has reached the hundred mark this season, for in the opening match for Halesowen Grammar School against Bromsgrove Grammar School, he contributed 150.'

"I was lucky that I could play for Worcestershire," Charles now says, "as my birthplace was Staffordshire, a second-class county. The regulations at that time permitted a player from a minor county to play for the nearest first-class county, providing there was no objection from the minor county. Well, my uncle had been captain of Staffordshire so that was no trouble for me. There was only one problem: how was I to take advantage of the privilege of going to Worcester? It was 25 miles away."

By the mid-1930s the Palmers had acquired a car, but Charles' father needed this for his work. Providentially there lived in The Crescent at Old Hill an old Surrey player George Platt, who had been professional at the local club before moving on to take up a position as coach at Worcester. "He had a little Morris Eight or something," Charles recalls. "It got us there and back."

George Platt had achieved little at The Oval, though he could boast a record-breaking return in Minor Counties competition when he took ten for 15 for Surrey Second Eleven against Dorset. "He wasn't a great player," says Charles, "and some people would say he wasn't a great coach, either. But I found that he had got that knack of finding what faults I had, and he was a good enough bowler to feed those faults and put them right."

OFF TO THE NETS.—Members of the Worcestershire C.C. have started practice. The team will be the first county side to meet the Australians this season. Here are (left to right) Grimshaw, C. H. Palmer, G. Platt (coach), Horton, Oakley and King going to the nets. *Birmingham Gazette photograph.*

Charles remembers the difficulties he had been experiencing after his years away from cricket in the war. "Somehow, when I came back to cricket after having been away, I found that I wasn't using as much of my offside repertoire as I had before. George Platt immediately spotted faults that had developed because I was playing round my front leg. And he was the sort of bowler who could bowl to order with accuracy. He bowled at me, something on the leg stump or just outside, or on middle stump, over after over after over, so he got me moving my left leg. Then I found I developed another shot because I could hit the ball on the onside as well as the offside. I liked George Platt and he certainly helped me."

Trips down to Worcester with Platt became part of Charles' routine in the Easter and summer holidays in his teens and, if he was playing in a match, his mother would come down to watch. This became possible because she could travel with her sister-in-law, Uncle Bert's wife, who had the use of a car. "My uncle was rather better heeled than my old man," says Charles. "He was the

21

managing director of Halesowen Steel Company, when steel was something." Like his mother, Charles' Aunt Ruby was an avid cricket watcher, and the two ladies also travelled together to watch Warwickshire, where they were members of the ladies' section.

In the autumn of 1937, now aged 18, Charles went to Birmingham University, where he read English, as his main subject, with Latin and Philosophy. By now he had decided that he fancied a career in teaching and this meant that he could take advantage of a scheme whereby, in committing to take a certificate of education after graduating, he received help with his fees.

Cricket continued to play an important part in his life, but the university's matches, where he played alongside RH Maudsley, later of Warwickshire, he recalls as pretty amateur affairs. He enjoyed success against the other universities but, he says, "Redbrick cricket was not very good."

Useful performances in colts matches and a century for the second eleven led Worcester to consider Charles for a place in the first team but, when his opportunity came in July 1938, he could scarcely have been less well prepared. "I was playing cricket down in South London when I got a telegram from the Secretary of Worcestershire, saying 'Can you be at Park Avenue, Bradford tomorrow morning by eleven?'"

Sid Martin, the county's South African all-rounder, had broken a finger in the match against Middlesex at New Road. A replacement was urgently needed, but there was still a problem: "How the hell could I get to Bradford by eleven o'clock? I'd got to go home and pick up kit and so forth."

Arriving back at Old Hill that evening, Charles still had no idea how he was going to tackle the next leg of the journey when a saviour materialised. Billy Edwards, a mad-keen cricket fan and President of Old Hill, lived opposite the Palmers. "He said, 'I'll drive him up.' We set off at five o'clock in the morning to get there. No motorways! He didn't deny himself – we went in his Rolls Royce; and we got as far as some place not far from Bradford where the Rolls Royce had a bit of an altercation with a church wall. I got out. There was only about half an hour to spare. We were on a bend, and people didn't particularly want to stop. Then a milk float came along, and I thought it was going slowly enough for me to halt it. The driver very kindly said, 'OK I'll take you to Park Avenue.'"

Much to his relief Charles reached the amateurs' dressing room shortly before the match was due to start, and there he joined the Hon CJ Lyttelton, the captain, and Mr CDA Pullan. Cecil 'Plug' Pullan, on holiday from the Gold Coast, was returning to the side after a three-year absence: "a useful player," Charles calls him, "but nothing special." Charles Lyttelton, however, was a more formidable character, later to become the 10th Viscount Cobham, President of MCC and Governor-General of New Zealand. In time he would become a personal friend, but "at that point I didn't really know him. We lived in different worlds. It was a time when aristocrats were aristocrats, and he was in the stratosphere."

The more familiar faces were in the professionals' dressing room. Some, like the 19-year-old Roly Jenkins, playing in only the second match of a career that would stretch to 1958, were familiar from Club and Ground matches, but the older players were just as welcoming. "Peter Jackson, Reg Perks and Dick Howorth, they were all very accommodating for a youngster coming into the side."

Worcestershire had won the toss and chosen to bat on a damp wicket.

"The captain, God bless him, had put me in at number four and I had a scramble to get my pads on. I sat down in fear and trepidation, but dear old Maurice Leyland came in, put his arm round me and said, 'Is this your first match, young 'un?' And I said 'Yes, sir, it is.' 'Get a few runs, but not too many of them'. That was the sort of attitude. There was a camaraderie in first-class cricket in those days."

After his rush to the ground, Charles was able to sit and experience the atmosphere of the first-class game. A wicket fell with the score on 25, but Eddie Cooper and Charlie Bull survived till lunch-time. Soon afterwards, with the total on 85, Cooper was dropped at deep square leg. Then on the same score Charlie Bull was lbw, and Charles was in.

"I can remember I walked out to the wicket in a daze, seeing all the Yorkshire players, who were almost all England players. And I knew they'd won the Championship almost every year since 1930." In fact, four of Yorkshire's Test men – Hutton, Verity, Smailes and Gibb – were assembling at Old Trafford for a Test that would never start, though Sutcliffe, Bowes, Leyland, Barber and Wood were all present to greet the incoming batsman as he prepared to face Ellis Robinson.

The 19-year-old debutant 'shaped confidently,' taking a couple of singles before off driving Robinson to the boundary. There was another cover-driven four. "Then Ellis Robinson, unusually, bowled me a long hop on this slow wicket. The biggest long hop you've seen in your life. My eyes popped out of my head, and I tried to belt it out of the ground." But Charles had chosen the longest boundary on the ground and there was the amateur GA Wilson, still smarting from having dropped Cooper. He would not repeat his mistake.

Mr CH Palmer, c Wilson b Robinson, 10. There was to be no second innings as rain moved in to prevent any play on the second and third days.

At Stourbridge, in the next match, Worcestershire needed 231 to beat Gloucestershire and, going in at number seven, Charles joined Cooper with the score on 72 for five. Reg Sinfield, 'bowling off-breaks in deadly fashion', had already taken eleven wickets in the match, but the Worcester pair took the score to 166 before Cooper was bowled and the innings folded up. Charles was left on 51 not out, and for 'Umpire', the columnist in the *Evening News and Times*, his innings was 'as promising a performance as I have ever seen by a newcomer to the first-class game. He showed that he has a keen eye, quick feet, a full repertoire of strokes and a sound judgment of the ball to hit and the one to leave alone.'

A week later at Edgbaston Charles made 19 and 21 against Warwickshire, dismissed both times by Old Hill's own Eric Hollies, and in the following match at Loughborough, in his first visit to Leicestershire, he hit 56 and partnered Charles Lyttelton, whose 162 was the only century of his first-class career.

In all, Charles played ten games for Worcestershire that summer, and a series of low scores in the final matches left him with a tally of 205 runs at an average of 14.64. It was a modest start, but it was sufficient for *Wisden* to write that 'C.H. Palmer gave indication of real skill.'

CHAPTER 3

THE FIND OF THE SEASON

When Charles arrived at Dudley on the morning of Saturday 10th June 1939, he had just completed his second year at Birmingham University and was reporting for his first county match of the summer.

Worcestershire were in the lowest of spirits. A fortnight earlier, in a motor accident near Chelmsford, their opening batsman Charlie Bull had been killed and their wicket-keeper Syd Buller seriously injured. The team was in shock, and the next three matches were all lost badly, with the batsmen struggling in vain to compile competitive totals.

Charles was fresh blood, bringing with him the promise of his first games the previous summer, but nobody at Worcester can have been prepared for the magnitude of his immediate success. Under blue skies, against Northants at Dudley, he hit 132 in two and a half hours. 'It was a delightful display,' according to *The Times*. 'He is a fine striker with an attractive style.' He followed this in his next innings, in damper and more difficult conditions at Cardiff, with a score of 128. From there he travelled to Edgbaston where his first innings 62 won him his county cap and, when he added a third century at Trent Bridge before the month of June was out, his name appeared in the first ten of the national batting averages, below Hammond, Compton, Hutton and Sutcliffe.

He scored 84 against Surrey at New Road, Worcester, 'another grand display of hard, clean hitting', and a week later came an innings at Old Trafford that he has never forgotten. He had pulled a thigh muscle and had Hugo Yarnold as his runner. "I was facing Eddie Phillipson. My God, was he quick that day! I think I must have had three gins at lunchtime or something because I went out wafting my bat at him and I hit him for a couple of fours. And I said to Hugo Yarnold, 'You know where the next one's coming – at my head!' But I was so cocky at that time, I went down the leg side to give myself room to play the same shot once more. But this time he saw me coming, and he honed in on me. Bonk! My head! In fact I was told by the medics that, if I hadn't had such a thick skull, it would probably have killed me."

Mr CH Palmer, retired hurt, 65 absent hurt, 0

After a week out of the game, Charles would return to find runs harder to come by. "I remember Doug Wright of Kent coming to Worcester. I used to go down the wicket to the spinners, but I made a mess of it occasionally. He bowled pretty fast, didn't he? Next thing I knew, I was back in the pavilion. And I thought, 'Well, that's my lesson. I'm not going down the track to him next time.' So I stayed back. Well, of course, I was pinned back on my stumps. Clean bowled, just like that! I remember going back home to my father and saying, 'If that's first-class cricket, I'm not going to make it.'"

Cricket writers thought otherwise. 'Young Palmer on the way to Test Class' boomed a headline in the *Sunday Dispatch*. Its columnist FG Reekie described the Worcestershire amateur as 'the find of the season … He has been booked by Sir Pelham Warner to appear in the Folkestone Festival.' Alas, with the outbreak of war, the Festival was cancelled, and Charles' cricketing progress was brought to an abrupt halt.

In his first appearances for Worcester Charles had occasionally worried that he was depriving a more deserving professional of his place in the side, but now he had established himself in his own right and he felt at ease in the company of the paid players. The social stratum in which he had grown up had more in common with the background of some of the professionals than with that of his companions in the amateurs' dressing room.

Nevertheless, in Charles' view, the distinction of amateur and professional was never a matter of much consequence at Worcester. "Rather different from Lancashire, Middlesex and Surrey. Surrey, in particular. I should imagine Somerset was another one where the amateur ethos was the only one. We had no worry about the amateur-pro distinction, provided the amateur was good enough for his place. But if he was brought in to save a bob or two and a pro was kicked out, of course the amateur quickly lost favour, and rightly so."

As a fellow amateur Charles grew to know Charles Lyttelton and his world, travelling from match to match as a passenger in his car, and they were joined in the amateur dressing room that summer by newcomer Allan White. "Allan had got so much money, he didn't have to do a damn thing. All he did was drink. He didn't drink himself silly, but he was partial to it. But I liked Allan."

Another perspective on the amateur ethos came from playing a few games with the Nawab of Pataudi, who had appeared in three Tests for England and would lead the Indian tourists to England in 1946. "I didn't really know him, but he was an extraordinary batsman. He was so elegant. He had all the Indian wizardry about him, and he was marvellous to watch, to be at the other end with. I've often described him as making me feel like an elephant because he was so graceful.

"Mark you, once he'd batted, he wouldn't field. He stayed in the dressing room. He turned to the privilege of an amateur and did not field, not while I played with him. He'd either got something wrong with him – or conjured something up."

Charles remembers Lyttelton as one of the game's great theorists, his swashbuckling style at the crease belying his more cerebral approach. "We had had CF Walters at Worcester, a beautiful player, and Charles Lyttelton based his theory of batting on him. He always maintained that, when you are playing a fast bowler, you don't get right behind the line, you get slightly to the off side. The old pros were having none of this. But after another batting collapse Charles Lyttelton said, 'You don't take any bloody notice of what I say. You keep getting out. I'll show you. I'll go in first.'

"Well, this match was against Derbyshire, sod's law, with Bill Copson, a lively performer, on a green wicket at Worcester. Charles put his theory into practice, and the third ball the off stump went past first slip. So he stalked back to the pavilion. He was born to the purple and had the language to go with it. All the pros, of course, knew what was going to happen. It was only one tiny little step from one dressing room to the other, and they'd heard it all before. 'Anyone can have that!' he would shout, and the bat would go right across the room.

"Reg Perks was the senior pro, and he decided he would go into the amateurs' dressing room and stand behind the door so that he couldn't be seen. When the bat went across and Charles said, 'Any stupid fool can have that.' Reg said, 'Thanks skipper', picked it up and walked out."

WORCESTERSHIRE'S YOUNG MEN

A "Sports Argus" snapshot of two Worcestershire cricket notables — C. H. Palmer, the young Old Hill and Birmingham 'Varsity player, who has scored centuries in two successive county matches, is on the left, and the Hon. Charles Lyttelton, the Worcestershire captain. Snapped this morning in the pavilion at Edgbaston, where Warwickshire are entertaining Worcestershire.

The young Charles had always planned to play county cricket as an amateur. "I had been brought up in an amateur environment," he says. Moreover, consorting with Lyttelton, Charles came to realise that there were material benefits to life as a gentleman cricketer. "You travelled first class on the train and, if there were some good seats going at the theatre, you got them ahead of the pros."

Through Lyttelton, Charles came to extend his circle of social contacts. He looks back on how, as a 20-year-old, he first met CP Snow, the novelist and scientist, the eldest of three brothers all with a passion for cricket. Eric would write the history of Leicestershire County Cricket Club, while Philip – a colonial administrator – was for many years at the heart of cricket in Fiji, where he created a multi-racial national side.

With his love of words, Charles was entranced by the erudite conversations of Lyttelton and CP Snow. "I used to listen in awe to fluent, golden verbal cascades sans pareil." In later years Charles and Lyttelton would often find themselves on the same toast list at cricket dinners. "He was a great raconteur and, whenever we were speaking together, I always stipulated that I should speak first. He was an impossible man to follow."

It seems that Lyttelton was already making arrangements for how he should be remembered. "He once told us that he had composed his own epitaph for display in the Hagley Hall burial ground. It ran:

Here I lie beneath this tump,
Bowled again, middle stump!"

He died in 1977, and some years later Charles visited Hagley in the hope that he would see his old captain's final bon mot. "We searched in vain. Perhaps the family thought it too trivial for a tenth viscount. But rumour had it that all was not lost and that a beloved sister had had the epitaph typed and put in the coffin."

Another distinguished novelist in the Lyttelton/Snow circle was Francis Brett Young. It was through the influence of Snow and Young that the possibility arose that Charles might move on from Birmingham University to St Catherine's College, Cambridge, where Snow was admissions tutor.

"Francis Brett Young wrote me a testimonial. My mother was always very assiduous as far as her son was concerned, and in those days she wouldn't have known what a photocopier was. So she copied it out in long hand, this letter from Francis Brett Young written on my behalf. I blush to read it really; it's a typical novelist who delights in words and has got to make the most of saying what a fine fellow Palmer was."

A two-year course at Cambridge, reading English again, would have provided Charles with the opportunity of winning a blue for cricket and, with MA (Cantab) after his name, he would have had a more impressive curriculum vitae with which to embark on a teaching career. "If you looked around the public schools of that day, you never found a headmaster who was not an Oxbridge man. It was almost a sine qua non that you had to be Oxford or Cambridge, which I wasn't. So I thought my chances of becoming a headmaster, even if I wanted to be one, were not very rosy."

None of this came to fruition. Like so many other young men of this period, Charles had plans that never saw the light of day – "because Mr Hitler turned up."

Charles returned to his final year at Birmingham. He had volunteered for military service in September 1939 but was advised that he would not be called up until April. He calculated that he would be serving in the Army before the final examinations came round, and as a result he did not apply himself greatly to his studies. "Then, when the time came for me to be called up, they wrote again saying, 'We shall not require you for another year.' I've never worked so hard in my life to make up the lost ground!"

To his relief Charles managed to put on enough of a spurt to be awarded a degree. "Only a 'two two', but I was very lucky to get one at all." He was not present to receive it – "It was awarded in absentia," – a Latin term that Charles still relishes – but, sixty-four years later, "when Leicester University were daft enough to award me an honorary degree, I made sure I turned up!"

C. H. PALMER

His Career and Future

By " Umpire "

The remarkable success of C. H. Palmer during the past three weeks has set cricket supporters all over the County, and farther afield, asking for further information about him.

WHO is he? Where is he from? Can he play regularly? What's he doing at Birmingham University? On all sides wherever one goes these and similar questions are fired, showing that, by his striking achievements, this young amateur has properly captured the hearts of cricket lovers.

Apart from the Nawab of Pataudi, who in his first season with Worcestershire made a habit of hitting double centuries instead of just centuries, Charles Palmer has achieved a greater and earlier success than any other Worcestershire amateur. Even C. F. Walters did not meet with such early success. Remember this is only Palmer's second season in first-class cricket, and the first was by no means a full one, for he only played in ten matches. This young student has yet to face established County bowlers who are complete strangers to him, which makes one ponder on what he might achieve if his progress is maintained during the next year or so, in which he will be gaining valuable experience.

Future Connection
With Worcestershire

AT the moment the most insistent question which is being asked concerns the likelihood of Palmer's future appearances for Worcestershire

If needed—and there can surely be no two opinions on that point—he will be available for the greater part of many seasons to come.

From Halesowen Grammar School Palmer, who is a gifted scholar, went to Birmingham University, whence he will enter the teaching profession. At the moment he is on vacation, which will continue until the end of the present cricket season.

As he is of militia age, he must between now and next year put in the required six months regular training, which interruption to his studies is expected to take place this winter, and which means that he will still be at the University next summer and until the end of the summer of 1941.

Whilst he is at the University he will be able to play in the first two or three matches of each season and then regularly from the middle of June onwards.

Nor should he be lost to Worcestershire when his University days are over for, as it is his intention to become a master at a public school he will be free during the long summer holidays.

So his future association with the County is reasonably assured for a long while.

His Early Promise

PALMER was born at Old Hill, Staffordshire, in a house 50 yards only from the Worcestershire borders. He became qualified for Worcestershire through being educated at Halesowen Grammar School, which is in Worcestershire, and by permission of Staffordshire, which was readily given.

As a boy at Old Hill, Palmer was always to be found playing at every available opportunity, and in those early days he impressed George Platt as having the early stamping of a future cricketer.

Then came the launching of the County's Nursery, and when George was appointed coach and a number of boys were being taken on, he suggested to Major Jewell and Mr. Lane that young Palmer was one who should be offered terms, with a view to joining the staff. Actually these approaches were made but the boy, who had made up his mind to

C. H. PALMER

enter the teaching profession, turned the proposal down—unfortunately for Worcestershire, it is true, but a wise decision on the part of a boy of 17.

I happen to know that this decision was a great disappointment to George Platt, who thereupon suggested that the boy should come for coaching during the holidays and play for the Colts.

Keen Interest Displayed

THIS opportunity young Palmer jumped at and each year since he has travelled to and fro between Old Hill and back. on every possible occasion.

George Platt estimates that, in order to avail himself of first-class practice, Palmer has made this journey 150 times in the past three years

This means that, in order to become an accomplished cricketer, he has travelled 7,800 miles for practice and coaching!

George's system of coaching, which is to take one stroke at a time and pass on to the next only when that one has been mastered, Palmer accepted without demur and the measure of success which he has already achieved must be a matter for considerable satisfaction to his tutor.

He made such rapid progress in these early days at Worcester that he went straight into the Colts' side and, having made several good scores with them, made his debut with the first team that year.

His subsequent success in premier cricket George attributes to the fact that he plays the ball late on the on-side and always tries to force it in front of the wicket, his strong play being off the back foot.

His Promise As An All-Rounder

AS is well-known, Palmer hit his first century in first-class cricket against Northants at Dudley three weeks ago to-day. But what is not known is that on the previous Thursday he had completed

GEORGE PLATT, the County coach, who thinks very highly of his pupils promise.

his examinations at the University, then spent the whole of Firday at the nets at Worcester before going to Dudley the next day.

It is, of course, as a batsman that Palmer has "hit the headlines" but he is also a very useful fielder in any position, which is a useful asset to a County side, and he is also quite a useful change bowler; he spins the ball and varies its pace well but as yet his length needs to be made more accurate.

As a young man, Palmer is of an unassuming nature. As a cricketer he seems to have a sound knowledge of the game—he was captain of cricket at Halesowen Grammar School and is Secretary of cricket at the University—and I think he will continue to give proof that he is the type of batsman which Worcestershire badly needs.

Palmer has already brought honour to Worcestershire. He has been invited to take part in the England "Past and Present" match in the Folkestone Festival at the close of the present season.

The Victory Over Gloucestershire

THE County's win over Gloucestershire was a creditable one but can anyone remember cricket as dull as that provided by the visiting County the first day? For the greater part it was of the type calculated to destroy interest in the first-class game—instead of encourage it which is what harassed County secretaries need at the moment.

Fortunately, in one respect, the cold weather kept the crowd down to a few hundreds, so that many who normally attend on a Saturday did not see this bad advertisement for the game.

Agreed the weather was not conducive to bright play, but one could not blame the conditions for batting which was as tedious as they were cheerless.

When Worcestershire batted they—or rather King. Gibbons and Cooper—afforded a direct contrast. If somewhat favoured at the start of his innings, King later was wholly delightful to watch, hitting all types of bowling with freedom and power. He richly deserved his first century of the season and, what is more, he came to Worcestershire's rescue in the second innings when, if defeat was not exactly threatening, things were not going at all well with two wickets down for four runs.

In hitting his fourth century of the season—for him a remarkable one of ups and downs—Gibbons revealed all his old immaculate skill

New Player On Trial

AT the moment the County have on trial a young batsman from the Central Lancashire League, J. Wood, who is with Werneth.

Wood took part in the Colts match this week against Warwickshire II. and hit a fine century in his second innings after getting twenty odd in the first.

He is 21 years of age and I saw part of his century knock and he gave the impression that he has the right temperament for the game, every confidence, a nice style and clean-cut strokes. I did not see him field but the County coach told me that he is a useful spin bowler and a splendid fielder.

Barbara

CHAPTER 4

AN EASY WAR

"I had an easy war," Charles admits as he looks back on five years spent in the South East of England, followed by a posting to India after the end of the conflict.

Charles was called up in September 1940, a year after he had first volunteered for service. He was commissioned into the Royal Artillery, rising to the rank of captain and being assigned to the Anti-Aircraft division. Based for most of the time in Sussex, he was comfortably billeted, and it was a bonus to find that he was in a battery that included women.

Their duty was to bring down enemy bombers and the dreaded doodlebugs as they came across the channel. "We didn't bring down as many as we ought to have done," Charles feels, "especially as the doodlebugs were travelling at a constant speed and a constant height. We ought to have blasted them out of the sky, but we were rotten shots!"

The doodlebugs, unpiloted flying bombs, announced themselves with a throbbing sound as they flew overhead. This was followed by a foreboding silence when the timing device cut out the engine, telling those on the ground below that they had only a few seconds to try and find shelter before the bomb would crash to earth and explode on impact.

"I recall one unforgettable piece of flying by a pilot of a Tempest. He flew with the wing of his plane under the wing of this doodlebug and gave it a nudge so that it was thrown out of equilibrium. The pilot had taken it out of the straight and narrow, but he got it to a situation where he thought that, if it did now go down, it would land in a congested area. So he went to the other side and straightened it out and gave it another nudge. It was the most wonderful bit of flying."

On 21st February 1942, the wedding took place between Charles and his old school friend Barbara Butler. They married in front of a small family congregation in the beautiful little church of St Kenelm's in the Worcestershire village of Clent, some four miles from where both families lived. "You would struggle to fit fifty people into it," Charles says, "but it was a fascinating place."

Romance had blossomed after Barbara had moved on from Halesowen Grammar School to Malvern Girls' College, and it had continued when Charles was studying at Birmingham University and she was working in a bank in the city. "We spent our entire life going to local dances," she says. "That's what everybody did in those days."

It was a winter wedding, arranged in the midst of war and with thick snow lying all round the church, but it has proved durable through all the seasons. After marriage Barbara also found herself serving in the ack-ack. She was stationed for a while in the beleaguered city of Coventry, so it was not till after the war that they were able to start a family. Andrew was born in 1947, Tim in

1950, and now there are five grandchildren as well as great-grandchildren.

One of the advantages of Charles' posting was that he was still able to play a few games of cricket. He represented the Army in a number of one-day matches, some of them at Lord's where the main ground and pavilion remained available for cricket, though the Nursery and many other buildings were requisitioned for military use.

On 29th July 1944 he was playing for the Army against the RAF at Lord's when the players heard the drone of a doodlebug cutting out above them. They all threw themselves to the ground, but the bomb came down in Regent's Park and the cricketers were unharmed. When play resumed, Jack Robertson celebrated by hitting the second ball he received for six.

Charles has little to add in the way of an eye witness report. "I didn't see much of that because we were batting and I was under the table in the home dressing room."

Another who played in the match was the Nottinghamshire batsman Charlie Harris. "He was a lovely man, whimsical and a very good player when he wanted to be. But he didn't want to play in these matches for the Army because he'd managed to get a job as a pro on Saturdays with some Lancashire team, where – if he gave a good performance – they took a collection. It could be up to forty or fifty pounds, a lot of money then. I remember batting with him when he was trying to avoid being picked for the Army. He'd pat a half-volley gently back to the bowler or tap a full toss to cover and each time he'd say, 'They'll not pick me for bloody Army again.'"

Charles also recalls that Harris once had the nerve to submit an expense claim to Sir Pelham Warner for a first-class fare from Scarborough to Lord's, while he was stationed at Woolwich. As the return fare to Lord's from Woolwich was no more than one shilling and eight pence, it was not a claim that Sir Pelham entertained.

The war in Europe ended in May 1945 and that summer, with the visit of an Australian Services team, there was time once more for three-day, first-class cricket. On 1st September Lord's staged a match in aid of the St Mary's Hospital Centenary Fund, and the two teams were 'elastically termed' Over 33 and Under 33. The 26-year-old Charles played for the Over 33s and, six years and one day after his previous first-class appearance, he provided the best entertainment of the first day with some 'delightful strokes' in an innings of 77. In the words of *The Times*, he was 'of undoubted quality. He scored at a good pace without ever giving the impression that he was hurrying.'

But, just as demobilisation was getting under way, with the prospect of more cricket and a proper family life, Charles found himself posted to India. He travelled out by sea, his first trip abroad, and, when he arrived, it seemed that there was little active service required of him. A diary started at the time reveals a life spent playing sport, eating rather better than he would have done in England and enjoying some of the night spots.

"When I got there they shoved me in a transit camp at Deolali, just outside

Bombay. I wasn't there for very long, but all the time I was picking up papers saying that Compton had got a hundred, then Compton had got another hundred. After a time I got a bit narked with this, sitting on my backside, doing nothing very interesting. So I wrote to Compton and I said, 'Hey, you seem to be playing a lot of cricket. What about me?'"

War had not brought a suspension of first-class cricket in India, and in the final years of the conflict Denis Compton – a Sergeant-Major in charge of fitness training in the Commandos – was the most prominent of a number of English professionals who appeared for the various Indian teams. In all, he played ten first-class matches in India, scoring seven centuries, and, before long, Charles, too, was "playing non-stop cricket."

On New Year's Day 1946 Charles left Deolali on a two-day journey to Calcutta. There he had no sooner arrived than he was in the nets at Eden Gardens, where his diary records that among those he met were Dickie Dodds, soon to become an Essex cricketer, and the Maharajah of Cooch Behar.

Three days and several good meals later the diary entry reads: 'Services XI 246. Palmer 116.' This was a match against a strong local team captained by the Test batsman Syed Mushtaq Ali, and as a result Charles was summoned to the other side of India to play for the Europeans in Bombay's Pentangular tournament. It would be his one first-class match in India.

Travelling the long distances around India invariably presented problems. It was seldom comfortable, "even if you had the red carpet laid out for you." Progress by train was stately rather than swift. Though there were sometimes restaurant cars, Charles remembers that "we stopped at many stations where they would have telephoned ahead that the train was coming and we'd want so many meals laid on for lunch. And when we got to the station, there they were on a big table, which was rather more civilised."

For many years the Bombay Pentangular had been India's foremost competition, with teams comprised of Hindus, Muslims, Parsees, Europeans and the Rest. With the Independence movement of the Indian people reaching its climax, there was much hostility to a competition called by one former Indian captain 'the canker of communal cricket', and this tournament in January 1946 would prove to be the last one held.

Gloucestershire's Bev Lyon was captain of the Europeans, and his side contained three men who were or would become Test cricketers: Denis Compton, Reg Simpson of Nottingham and Charles. But in the first round match against the Hindus, despite 91 and 124 from Compton, they were dismissed for only 212 and 291 and lost by an innings. Charles was bowled for 12 and run out for 21.

Reg Simpson was in the RAF. He had completed his operational training in England in late 1944 and had found to his dismay that only those with surnames A to P were to be to be posted to English stations. He was off to India. "Now Reg, do be careful," his anxious mother pleaded as she said goodbye. "Don't fly too high, will you?"

"I played my first first-class game while I was waiting to be posted to my squadron," Reg recalls. "I wandered into Karachi to try to find out about cricket, and eventually I played quite a bit there. I was picked for Sind to play against Maharastra in the Ranji Trophy. I've been tickled since to see in *Wisden* that they list me as playing for 'Sind and Notts', so everybody thinks I'm a Pakistani!"

The Europeans, versus The Hindus, Bombay, January 1946

left to right: Fred Eccleston, Charles Palmer, Roland Ingram-Johnson,
Peter Judge, Peter Brayshay, Bev Lyon, Rainy Brown, Reg Simpson,
Paul Dobree-Carey, Denis Compton, Aubrey Sinden

Reg and Charles quickly became good friends, and one evening during the Pentangular match they accepted an invitation to join their captain for dinner at the Taj Mahal hotel. "We went thinking it was a table for three. When we got there, it was a table for 48. And then somebody on our table recognized the Aga Khan in another party, and we were swimming in champagne for the rest of the evening."

Charles had tried his hand at many sports and at school his principal winter game had been rugby, but he had been too small to be effective in the adult game. Early in his military service he had been pressed to turn out for his unit side and he had done so with no great expectation of success. "They said, 'We'll put you on the wing.' I thought I'd got through the game without being crucified when, just before the end, somebody gave me the ball about the length of this room away from the line. I thought, 'Palmer, you can go out in a blaze of glory and score a try in your last game.'

"But what I hadn't noticed was that, as I was going for the line, Vivian Jenkins, the Welsh international full back, was coming towards me. I was waiting for the crunch. But he didn't tackle me; with one hand he picked me up and put me on the other side of the line so I couldn't score a try."

As a rugby player, Charles had had no experience of soccer, so it came as a big surprise when a senior officer at GHQ approached him. "He said to me out of the blue, 'Would you like to manage some professional soccer stars?' I'd never played soccer in my life, but I said, 'I don't mind.'"

For the next few weeks Charles managed the Inter-Services Sports Exhibition side, travelling around India and Ceylon with a team that included several future internationals, among them Johnny Morris of Manchester United, Tottenham goalkeeper Ted Ditchburn and the Welsh wing-half Ivor Powell. "We went all over the place from Madras to Hyderabad. We toured wherever there were forces. And we had to arrange to lose to the local unit side once in a while."

For one journey, from Colombo to Delhi, Charles was surprised to find their plane piloted by Reg Simpson. "When he heard that I'd never been in a cockpit, he installed me in the co-pilot's seat. It was fascinating. We climbed to about 3,000 feet and looked down, and I turned to Reg to ask a question. But he wasn't there! I had never heard of George, the automatic pilot, and I just managed to survive the moments of terror until Reg returned to the pilot's seat.

"He gave me a blanket and I made myself comfortable on the floor for this long flight. We travelled as planned to Bombay, Karachi and Jodhpur, by which time it was dark and I was asleep. Then I was awakened by a bellow from Reg. In our cricket he had always seemed imperturbable, even against the most hostile bowling, but now he was agitated and bathed in perspiration.

"Obviously there were major problems. We had run into the mother and father of all storms, and all his communication had failed. We could neither see nor speak to anyone. Reg decided to make a square search, but we were now flying blind and fuel was getting perilously low. It was only in the nick of time that communication was restored. Otherwise there would have been press reports that a whole football team and a couple of cricketers had crash-landed in the Sind Desert."

"We'd turned and gone back to Jodhpur," Reg explains. "Luckily I had put on extra fuel because I thought there might be trouble with the storms. But, when we should have arrived back and didn't, that's when I started the square search. And eventually, just in time, I saw a white light ahead, the first light you could see in the middle of the Sind Desert. And at the same time the wireless operator got through. I remember Charles saying, 'I never knew flying a Dakota could be such hard work.'"

Charles was about to set off for the Dutch East Indies with his footballers when he was struck down with jaundice. After three weeks in hospital, he was demobbed and in May he began the boat journey home. 'Got caught by the sun taking photographs,' his diary records on the day of departure, then it goes blank for five days.

He had had an easy war in England, and his posting to India had been a long round of sport and socialising. He had enjoyed seeing a new continent, but he had had little contact with the great changes that were taking place politically. "The only time we felt the build up of the Partition business was when we'd be making a journey and we couldn't get through to the station for all the demonstrations in favour of independence."

At Port Suez their boat refuelled and picked up more passengers. Then the following day, at Port Said, his diary contains its final entry. 'Cinema show Constant Nymph, but walk out – conditions bad.'

It was time to return to Barbara and to start earning a living.

CHAPTER 5

TEACHING AT BROMSGROVE

Charles took stock of his situation. He was a married man, a place at Cambridge was no longer a realistic option, and he began to wonder how he might pick up the threads of life out of uniform.

"At the end of the war people said, 'What are you going to do now?' I said, 'I haven't a clue.' I wasn't vocationally trained, I hadn't got a certificate of education, I hadn't done an apprenticeship; in other words, I'd done bugger all except pick up a degree in English, which wasn't the greatest qualification of all time to earn a lot of money."

During the war Charles had been stationed with AL Warr, an England rugby international who had kept wicket occasionally for Oxford in the early 1930s. Educated at Bromsgrove School, he had returned there to teach.

Schools were looking anxiously for young men who might take up teaching posts, and at Bromsgrove a vacancy had arisen when Roger Human, their master in charge of cricket, had been killed in war service. "This chap Warr said to me, 'Are you interested in doing that sort of job, running the cricket and teaching a bit of Latin and English?' Well, having had six years in the war, I said I was interested in anything that would give me a crust. So he said, 'I'll fix up an interview with the Headmaster of Bromsgrove to see if he might be interested in you replacing Roger Human.' I said, 'Over to you, you do what you think is best.'"

The meeting with the Headmaster, David Walters, took place unconventionally at Lord's. "We had the interview in the Long Room, with my pads on. The first thing he said was, 'Have you got a certificate of education?' I thought, 'That's blown it.' Then to my delight he said, 'Thank God, that means I don't have to unlearn you everything you've learnt wrong.' So I went there to teach, and I thoroughly enjoyed myself for three years."

"David Walters backed his judgment with people," says Michael Roberts, a pupil in the 1940s.

"He was a super guy," says Charles. "He really was." It is a judgment that is endorsed by Charles' life-long friend Guy Jarrett, a classics scholar now 90 years of age, who also joined the staff in 1946 and spent the rest of his teaching career at the school. "An excellent man, the best headmaster there's been," he says, going on to recall the battle Walters had fought to keep the school alive in the grim years of the war.

"He was told, I think at the time of Munich, that, if war were to come, Bromsgrove School would be taken over for one of the Whitehall ministries; but he wasn't allowed to tell anyone this. So he had a look around for somewhere in case this awful thing happened and, being a Welshman, he thought of Wales and discovered a hotel in Llanwrtyd Wells. And that's where the school went. War came on September 3rd and they had to go at the beginning of term. So there was very little notice; it was up sticks and away."

The disruption of the move, coming at a time when the armed forces were claiming many of the best teachers, led to a fall in pupil numbers. The future of the school was threatened but, according to Guy Jarrett, David Walters was not prepared to countenance its closure. "Without telling anybody, he came back one day to Bromsgrove to look around the old school, and he found that two of the buildings were not being used at all. In another one that was being used, there was no sign of anyone and he found a notice on the wall: 'Baths will not be taken during office hours.' He took the notice down, roared up to Whitehall and said, 'What do you think about this misuse of my school?' And as a result the school came back. He told me that himself."

The return to Bromsgrove took place in 1943, and numbers soon began to build up again. By the time Charles arrived, there were about 300 boys in the senior school.

Barbara and Charles were housed in the school grounds in a 16th century cottage, overlooking fields with cattle and horses. "It was a lovely little spot, and we used to be woken up by the munch, munch, munch of a horse eating from the apple tree; but in 1947, which was the coldest winter of all time, we soon found that a 16th century cottage was not exactly hermetically sealed."

Charles taught English and was entrusted to do so to the Sixth form, supplementing this with some Latin classes in the preparatory school. "At the lowest possible level," he chuckles. "I didn't aspire to tread on Jarrett's toes in the upper school!"

It is on the sports field that he is best remembered. Here his friendship with Guy Jarrett soon blossomed, with the two men's wives also becoming great friends. In summer Jarrett would help Charles with the cricket and, when winter came, he would run the hockey with Charles' assistance; then on Saturdays the two men would play hockey together for Worcester, Charles on the right wing with Jarrett behind him at centre half or right half.

Guy Jarrett, a fine squash player and an Oxford Blue at Rugby fives, would probably have played international hockey, had it not been for the war. "I played in the last two England hockey trials before the war and one trial after the war, when I was probably too old for it. So it was a case of so near and yet so far."

Charles recalls the problem that he and Guy had one year with a young captain of cricket whose playing ability outstripped his tactical nous. "This chap became captain, faut de mieux, and we said, 'How are we going to get him to sort things out?' I said, 'I'll have a word with him.' So I said, 'Here's your opening bowler, that's your other opening bowler. Now this is the field that I want you to have.' And I wrote it all down. Then Jarrett and I were looking out from the pavilion, and we saw the most extraordinary field that he'd set. And eventually we said, 'What the hell's going on out here? You've got the drawing, haven't you?' Well it transpired he'd got the damn thing upside down!"

Then there was the time that Allan White was not engaged with a match for Worcestershire and came down to Bromsgrove to play with Charles and Guy Jarrett against the school. "Allan was a great extrovert, and his language was absolutely marvellous. He'd got every swear word under the sun. It was very muddy that day, and we were just hoping that he would restrain himself if something untoward happened during the game. Guy and I didn't really want the boys to hear all the expletives that he knew. And Allan absolutely amazed us because he took a toss on this very, very muddy ground and his face went into the mud, and we were waiting for all the effing to come out when he regained the perpendicular; and to his eternal credit he never said a word!"

On the aspiring cricketers who would bowl to him in the nets or in practice games in the middle, Charles made a lasting impression at Bromsgrove. Michael Roberts recalls, "He would adjust his specs, adjust his straw hat, then he'd put his forefinger and thumb to his jaw, step back, take his stance and away he'd go. There was a magical sense of timing, all wrist work; he never seemed to be hitting the ball hard. When he batted in the middle, it seemed that he was using his time there to give us all fielding practice."

For Nigel Sisson, who would captain the school team in the year when Charles had moved on to Leicestershire, an abiding memory is "of him peering down the pitch at you over his glasses rather like Ronnie Corbett, wrinkling his nose and making some terse comment. That's the picture that comes to me."

There was one terse comment that hit home to the young Sisson: "I remember once I played a match in coloured socks, which I shouldn't have done of course but I'd probably lost the white ones. Charles was umpiring, as schoolmasters tended to do, and I was out quite quickly, an appalling sort of knock, and as I went past he said, 'Serves you right, Sisson, you shouldn't wear blue socks.'"

Charles has never ranted and raved, but an unconfrontational style did not impair his ability to impose discipline. "You know which of your colleagues are having problems," Guy Jarrett says. "I don't think there's any doubt about that. Whether the headmaster also knows is a different matter. He stands less chance of knowing than the other members of the staff. I think, if Charles had had any trouble like that, we would have known. I can't believe he would have done because he had plenty of character."

To Michael Roberts, as a teenager approaching manhood, Charles was the kind of individual he had looked up to. "What more of an icon could you have?" For Nigel Sisson, young Mr Palmer was a breath of fresh air in the cloistered atmosphere of school life. "On a summer evening, after we had done all our work and played our games, Charles could be seen practising his golf, either long hitting or chipping down on the playing fields; and it was very relaxing to realise that people like him played other games as well."

"We were all very proud of him; he was ours," Nigel Sisson says. "We all felt like that, and we were slightly awed by his success. We all wanted him to succeed. But isn't it funny how he was remembered at the time not as Charles Palmer but as Charlie Palmer? I remember thinking it wasn't quite right. Charlie is a slightly musical hall sort of thing, and Charles was anything but music hall. He was better than that. He was very droll and very dry."

At the end of each summer term, Charles would head off to play for Worcestershire and the boys would look in the newspaper for his scores. There had been little of note in the summer of 1946 before Charles joined the staff at Bromsgrove, but the next year their cricket master was hitting the headlines, top of the county's averages and scoring two centuries, the highest 177 against Nottinghamshire at Dudley. "And he'd lost his kit," Mike Roberts recalls. "He did it with borrowed kit." Charles' own memory is hazy. "I made 177, I can remember that, but who it was against I haven't the faintest idea. I know we travelled somewhere by train, and it went straight through with my kit on it. Anyway I hadn't got any kit, and I had to play without my kit for a little while. That's rather Comptonesque, isn't it?"

The next summer opened with the famous 85 against the Australians. Guy Jarrett remembers his friend's form at the start of term at Bromsgrove: "All the boys who bowled at him and all the masters who thought they could bowl a bit, bowled at him. And I don't honestly think any of us could bowl anything he couldn't hit for four. He was in the most incredible form.

"But we watched him as the term went on, when he was out of practice for first-class cricket, and he lost this brilliance. I could occasionally bowl him a ball that made him defend."

Charles was away from Bromsgrove School in the winter of 1948/49, touring South Africa. Then, after a summer term at the school, he again went off to play for Worcestershire. Though he scored more than 700 runs in his summer holiday, at an average of 40, his freshest memory is of his first day back with the county, when Middlesex were the visitors and he spent all day in the field. With a Test match in progress, he opened the bowling, relieved that neither Compton nor Edrich was waiting to bat, but by close of play they were still bowling at the opener Jack Robertson, whose 331 remains to this day the highest score ever made for Middlesex.

"After tea," Charles recalls, "Allan White completely lost interest. He came out and nobody knew what positions to take up. I said, 'Where do you want me to go?' So he told me – in no uncertain terms!"

That summer the Worcestershire captaincy was shared by Allan White and the former England captain Bob Wyatt, now 48 years old.

"Allan was a nice chap, but he wasn't as hard a captain as Bob Wyatt. Bob was a very sound, thinking cricketer. He was a serious man; he taught me a lot. Mind you, I wouldn't have wanted to play like him because he was quite happy to stay there all day, whether he got runs or not. Of course he was sorted out by Martindale and Constantine in the West Indies; he had his jaw broken. But rumour has it that, as he was being taken away on a stretcher to the hospital, he called for someone and said, 'I don't want you to go in number six, I want you to go five.'"

A week after the Middlesex match, Worcestershire won victories both home and away against Hampshire. At Worcester, thanks to a fighting fifty by Wyatt himself, they scrambled home by one wicket, and in the next match at Portsmouth they won by seven wickets with a stylish 87 from Charles. At that stage they were top of the championship table, with only six matches to be played. Alas they won only two of them, finishing in third place, but it was nevertheless the county's best season since they had finished second equal in a much smaller programme of matches in 1907. *Wisden*, drawing particular attention to 'the solidity to the middle batting' provided by 'the talented amateur C.H. Palmer', reckoned that they might have won the title, had they always been able to field their strongest eleven.

MCC tour party, South Africa, 1948/49

Back row (from left): Jack Young, Roly Jenkins, Jack Crapp,
Allan Watkins, Bill Ferguson (Baggage Master)
Middle row: Godfrey Evans, Doug Wright, Cliff Gladwin, Alec Bedser,
Maurice Tremlett, Reg Simpson, Charles Palmer
Front row: Brigadier Michael Green (MCC manager), Cyril Washbrook, Billy Griffith,
George Mann, Len Hutton, Denis Compton, DJ Mentjies (South African manager)

CHAPTER 6

A WINTER AWAY FROM THE RATION BOOKS

> Aird is looking into extra coupons. As soon as he gets back from holiday, I will be writing to you.

The letter from MCC Secretary, Colonel RS Rait Kerr, informing Charles of his selection as one of the party to tour South Africa, ran to only three short paragraphs. Yet it found time for the important news that, in a country where rationing and restrictions were still the rule, the Assistant Secretary was doing his best to lay his hands on the precious clothing coupons that would allow the players to travel properly equipped for a tour that was to last six months.

Ronnie Aird returned from his holiday. 'Clothing coupons will be sent to you in due course,' he wrote cheerfully, but his next letter revealed the extent of his difficulties:

> My attempts to obtain clothing coupons from the Board of Trade have so far failed except for an allowance of 30 coupons per man for personal clothing for use during the voyage. Any coupons in addition to these will have to be supplied from a small reserve which I have at Lord's. Will you please let me know your minimum requirement?

Despite this lack of coupons, the MCC urged them to include in their packing 'dress clothes (ie dinner jacket and black tie), a warm suit and overcoat.'

"Why did we require a heavy suit?" Charles now wonders. "They gave us blazers that were made out of 22 ounce serge."

For the amateurs there was an allowance of £150, 'paid according to the English value of the pound', to cover 'drinks, tobacco and taxis to and from the grounds and all other incidental expenses.' "And that's for six months," Charles stresses, though he remembers one concession: "We were allowed one telephone call at Christmas."

Their contracts included restrictions preventing the players from speaking to the press. "They ought to have that now," he says. "All these people writing books and articles and what have you, I don't like it. I'm old-fashioned."

There was a farewell dinner at Lord's on Wednesday 6th October. Next day, they caught the boat train from Waterloo. There were 16 players in the party, four of whom – the captain George Mann, his deputy Billy Griffith, Charles and his wartime friend Reg Simpson of Nottinghamshire – comprised the amateur contingent MCC had been so keen to include. Charles and Reg Simpson would share a hotel room throughout the tour, but the ethos of the day decreed that the amateurs should be assigned single cabins on the boat.

Worcestershire's Secretary, Brigadier Green, travelled as manager with only Bill Ferguson, baggage man and scorer, to assist him. "He was one of the first to do the diagram scoring," Charles recalls. "They were works of art."

S.	M.	T.	W.	T.	F.	S.
5	6	7	8	9	10	11

5th — At Johannesburg.

6th — Dep. 9/30 a.m. Hotel by bus for Benoni. Match against North-Eastern Transvaal. Dep. By bus from the grounds after the match on direct run to PRETORIA. Stay at Polley's Hotel, where dinner is served.

7th } 8th } — Match against Combined Transvaal XI.

9th — Dep. 9/10 a.m. Motor from hotel to railway station. Dep. 9/40 a.m. PRETORIA by train. Arr. 11/12 a.m. JOHANNESBURG. Motor to and stay at Luthje's Langham Hotel. Match against Transvaal.

10th } 11th }

S.	M.	T.	W.	T.	F.	S.
12	13	14	15	16	17	18

12th — At Johannesburg.

13th — Match against Transvaal.

14th — Motor from hotel to railway station. Dep. 3/30 p.m. 4/30 p.m. JOHANNESBURG by train.

15th — Arr. 9/00 a.m. DURBAN. Motor to and stay at Hotel Edward.

16th } 17th } 18th } — First Test against South Africa.

SUBURBAN STREET, PRETORIA. The imposing beauty of Pretoria, the administrative capital of South Africa, is greatly enhanced by its colourful jacaranda-lined streets.

JOHANNESBURG SKYLINE. Spinning on a hub of gold, Johannesburg has grown from a mining camp on the bare veld to one of the greatest and richest cities in Africa.

DECEMBER

S.	M.	T.	W.	T.	F.	S.
19	20	21	22	23	24	25

DECEMBER

19th		At Durban.
20th		First Test against South Africa.
21st	3/30 p.m.	Motor from hotel to railway station.
	4/30 p.m. Dep.	DURBAN by train.
	11/35 p.m. Arr.	LADYSMITH. Motor to and stay at the Royal Hotel.
22nd } 23rd }		Match against Northern Districts of Natal.
24th	11/00 p.m.	Motor from hotel to railway station.
	11/40 p.m. Dep.	LADYSMITH by train.
	9/00 a.m. Arr.	JOHANNESBURG. Motor to and stay at Luthje's Langham Hotel.
25th		At Johannesburg.

JANUARY

S.	M.	T.	W.	T.	F.	S.
26	27	28	29	30	31	1

DECEMBER

26th		At Johannesburg.
27th 28th 29th 30th		Second Test against South Africa.
31st	6/50 a.m.	Motor to airport.
	8/15 a.m. Dep.	JOHANNESBURG by air.
	12 noon Arr.	CAPE TOWN. Airways' conveyance to railway station, then motor to Arthur's Seat Hotel, Sea Point.
1st		Third Test against South Africa.

LUXURY ROAD TRAVEL. Leaving the Royal National Park, famed mountain resort in the lee of the Drakensberg range, an S.A.R. de luxe bus heads for Ladysmith, en route to Durban.

MAN-MADE MOUNTAIN. Monuments to the endeavour of man in his search for gold are the white and yellow mine dumps dotted along the Rand.

The press party numbered about half a dozen, and Charles recalls that it included Alex Bannister *(Daily Mail)*, Charles Bray (*Daily Herald*), Reg Hayter (*Press Association*), Frank Rostron (*Daily Express*), EW Swanton (*Daily Telegraph*) and Crawford White (*News Chronicle*). Charles would grow to know these men well, not least when they would all be with him five years later when he was the manager in the West Indies.

"Delightfully few," says Charles. "They were out there doing their job of reporting cricket back to England. They weren't bothered with finding out who was in bed with whom. They were first-class; they didn't betray us, and they didn't betray themselves."

"It was a delightful tour," Charles says, "marvellously led by George Mann. As a captain he was ideal, and he was wonderfully well supported by Billy Griffith." Charles carries only the very happiest memories of a party where all the players got on well together and where the two teams mixed socially. For the smooth running of the tour, on and off the field, he pays tribute to Brigadier Green.

Memories of the trip are the fresher for Charles having preserved so many moments with a movie camera. For many years the film, a mixture of colour and black and white, had lain hidden away, almost forgotten, until a chance discovery of the old spools led to them being transferred to video in 2001.

Charles had had little filming experience before setting off to South Africa, but he had been approached on a train journey to London by a friendly passenger, who lent him a 16mm clockwork cine-camera. In the hands of the self-confessed amateur, it enabled Charles to capture the delights of the country and some shots of the cricket, though to his embarrassment the only time that the fall of a wicket was recorded was when he passed the camera to a female spectator when he himself went in to bat!

"For all we players, World War Two was only too fresh in the memory. Everyone associated with the cricket world, whether consciously or not, saw the tour as a means of returning to the normality of the life they had lost for six years." Thus does Charles' commentary start on the video; and the team soon found that South Africa contrasted pleasantly with the ration book life they had left behind.

Only on the field were there disappointments for Charles. When the party left England, it was clear that three batting places in the Test side were reserved for Hutton, Washbrook and Compton, while the captain would be at number six. With Evans as wicket-keeper and four bowlers, there were two places available for other batsmen, and four of the party would be scrapping for them: Jack Crapp, who had played in three of the summer's Tests against the Australians, another left-hander, Allan Watkins, who had made his debut at The Oval, and the two young amateurs, Reg Simpson and Charles.

Commentators had considered Watkins lucky to have been selected for the tour. Still to make much of a mark as a bowler, he was a world-class close fielder but, like Simpson and Charles, he had a batting average in the 20s for the 1948 season whilst, among those left behind in England, Jack Robertson and Arthur

Fagg had both exceeded 50. Charles, of course, was riding on his remarkable innings against the Australians, while Simpson had also distinguished himself against the tourists with a pair of seventies for Nottinghamshire.

Simpson, Watkins and Crapp all made runs early in the tour, but by the end of November Charles had played in three first-class matches and made scores of 0, 10, 14 not out, 13 and 0. "I couldn't get a run early on. I started by getting out in every sort of known way. Just one of those things. Allan Watkins had one or two jolly good innings, and on a tour, unless you cash in early, you've lost your chance, particularly with a batting side like we'd got over there."

His final chance in a first-class match before the selection of the side for the first Test came at Benoni, where the tourists were to play a weak North-Eastern Transvaal side. It was a match enlivened by an extraordinary display from Denis Compton, whose triple century remains the fastest in the history of first-class cricket. "It was an astonishing innings: 300 in three hours, one minute. Well, he could never be punctual for anything."

Compton's arrival at the wicket had come with the departure of Charles. "The main difference between his innings and mine was the mere matter of 300 runs."

Wisden records of Compton, 'Often he walked down the pitch before the bowler released the ball and he mixed orthodoxy with a bewildering assortment of unclassified strokes which went from the middle of the bat at lightning speed.'

"I remember, at a meeting of the team's Saturday Club, where fines were imposed for sundry 'offences', we passed a proposal to fine Denis a pound or two for doing that day what was by universal consent beyond the bounds of human achievement. He didn't know what we were talking about!"

The same match at Benoni saw Charles' Worcestershire colleague, leg-spinner Roly Jenkins, taking eleven wickets in only 29 eight-ball overs to complete a two-day victory. It was Jenkins' fifth match of the tour, four of them first-class, and already his wicket tally had reached 49.

"We played a lot together, Roly Jenkins and I. He was a great character. There were times when one thought he was a little bit unstable, but he was a damn good cricketer and he was a great trier. He was absolutely invaluable for these up country matches where you'd got not quite such good batsmen. He'd run through a side and let you go home quickly."

The first Test was played at Durban, a city where the team was always conspicuously well looked after. Charles remembers the reception when they had stayed there three weeks earlier for the Natal match. "We arrived at eight o'clock in the morning after an overnight journey, somewhat weary and unkempt. The chap who was organising us at Durban said, 'I hope you don't mind but, rather than go outside the front of the station, we'll take you out at the back.' We asked why. He said, 'Well there's rather a lot of press and people who want to say hello; great queues of people who want to talk to Denis Compton.' We said, 'How considerate of you.' And so we went to the back of the station so that we could go straight to our hotel, where we could open the mail and so forth. We were taken, in groups of three, in great shining American limousines. This is 1948, you couldn't even get a Morris Minor second hand over here, and these limousines were laid on to take us around Durban."

Nor were there only limousines. Each group was assigned an attractive female driver, whose presence enhanced the team's stay and provided a photo opportunity for the press corps – and a cutting preserved in Charles' scrapbook. As he looks at it, there is a twinkle as his eye alights upon one of the ladies. "Denise Chicken," he says, relishing the improbable name but saying no more. Another of the chauffeuses would soon become the second Mrs Denis Compton.

MCC's drivers

Miss L. Keyter, Miss Valerie Wood (later Mrs Denis Compton), Miss Frances Harris, Mrs Deryk Franklyn, Miss Denise Chicken, Miss Sonia Rosholt, Miss Pat de Gersigny

It was on one of their three visits to Durban that Charles recalls returning to the Edward Hotel in some disarray. "There were a couple of South Africans, George Mann, Billy Griffith and me. We weren't exactly sober and, as we drew up at the hotel at about two in the morning, Billy Griffith climbed out of the taxi and onto the roof, jumped off and fell in a big heap and said, 'My parachute didn't work!'

"Following Billy Griffith into the hotel was George Mann, and there was this doddery old night porter who was woken up by these wretched cricketers coming in. George did a rugby tackle on this old boy and he went down. It demanded a little bit of hush money."

The team entered the first Test undefeated, having won most of their matches by a comfortable margin and with the premier batsmen all in superb form. "If I had to choose someone to bat for my life, I think it would be Len Hutton," Charles says. "His defence was impregnable, and he could attack as well. His off driving seemed to have a divine inevitability about it, and with each shot we sank deeper and more complacently into our chairs. With Compton we all sat on the edge of our chairs saying, 'How on earth do you play that shot?'"

The Tests were all of four days' duration, and the first was played on the same Durban strip as the timeless Test of 1938/39, when after ten days England – chasing 696 for victory – had reached 654 for five, only to leave the game abandoned as a draw because they had a boat to catch. Now, ten years later, the batsmen struggled throughout the match. South Africa, batting first, managed only 161. England, thanks to Hutton and Compton, replied with 253. Then, when South Africa were bowled out for 219, England had just two and a quarter hours to score 128 for victory.

They soon lost valuable minutes when a shower drove the players from the pitch, and in persistent drizzle and poor light it was not an easy task. Even Compton, top scorer with 28, found runs hard to come by as 19-year-old Cuan McCarthy, in *Wisden's* words, 'maintained pace, length and hostility in a splendid spell of eighty-five minutes, in which, by taking six wickets for 33 runs in ten overs, he brought South Africa to within an ace of victory.'

Charles was not selected for the match so he could concentrate on capturing the final dramatic moments with his cine camera. With one eight-ball over remaining to be bowled, England were eight wickets down with eight runs still needed for victory and the batsmen at the crease were both tail-enders, Alec Bedser and Cliff Gladwin. "Cometh the hour, cometh the man," the latter had famously said as he made his way to the wicket.

The bowler for that last over was Lindsay Tuckett, a fast-medium right-armer with a lazy, lolloping approach to the wicket. Bedser worked a single off his first ball, then Gladwin sent the second with an agricultural heave to the square leg boundary.

As the village green stroke sailed over Eric Rowan's head, the match tilted England's way. "If Rowan hadn't moved in he would have caught it," says Charles. "But he was so excited and wanted to get into the match that he moved in 20 or 30 yards nearer the batsman, and that probably cost them the match." The camera next recorded a snick to fine leg for a single; then there was a powerful stroke from Bedser, but no run. On the fifth ball the South Africans appealed for lbw. Not out, but no chance of a run. The sixth ball finally brought a single and, with the scores level, Gladwin was back on strike.

In 130 years of Test cricket the finish of this Durban match ranks among the most dramatic, and probably the only camera in the ground recording the final over was that of the amateur cine-man Charles Palmer. But, alas, just as his film reaches the final climactic moments, the screen goes blank.

"I was so consumed with excitement that this is where my competence with the clockwork camera failed me. The last two balls, I pressed the trigger on the camera and the battery, or the clockwork, or whatever it was, hadn't wound up and I failed to get the historic picture."

So our only surviving record is of the voice of John Arlott in the commentary box:

> Two balls to go. Lindsay Tuckett's bowling to Gladwin. And it's a bouncer and it's outside the leg stump, and Wade in an attitude of prayer prevents it from being byes. And the next one they've got to run whatever happens. Tuckett from the Umgeni end to Cliff Gladwin. One run to win, and one ball to go. Tuckett to Gladwin. *(Hoarsely)* And he's knuckled it … and they're running … and Bedser isn't run out … and they've won on the last ball of the last over.
>
> And any sane man would tell you that England have won by two wickets. If you wanted to put it in a book, no one would ever believe it. It belongs to a novel, not *Wisden*. Never in all my life have I imagined that I would see such a finish.

In fact, the ball came off Gladwin's thigh, not his knuckle. Whichever way, the scrambled run brought England a victory that remains the only instance in the history of Test cricket when a side has snatched victory off the last possible ball.

On Christmas Eve they relaxed at a performance of *Oklahoma* by a visiting American company, and this was followed by a buffet supper with ham, tongue and turkey in proportions more lavish than had been seen for years in England, where most meat came out of tins. Then, before lunch on Christmas Day, the South African Broadcasting Association arranged for each of the tourists to send a message home.

"It really made me cry," Barbara remembers. "Because of his voice. I always thought he had a lovely voice, Charles. To hear his voice on the phone at Christmas was murder. I think I cried in my bedroom at home so my mother couldn't hear me crying, feeling sorry for myself."

Left alone with young Andrew, Barbara had not found life easy, but she had coped. "I came from a family where you were not allowed to moan about that kind of thing. But it was a hell of a long time, nearly eight months. Charles was away so long that the school asked me if I would mind somebody joining me in the cottage, another master and his wife. It could have been disastrous, but it wasn't, happily. And they used to sit in for me so I could get out at night sometimes."

On 27th December the second Test began. It was the first to be played at the rugby football ground at Ellis Park, Johannesburg. A high-scoring match, remembered for Hutton and Washbrook's record opening stand of 359, it ended in a dull draw on the evening of 30th December. Then the third Test started 800 miles away on New Year's Day at Cape Town, where unenterprising South African cricket left the home side unable to build upon their early advantage. 'A creeping paralysis seemed to settle upon some of them,' RJ Hayter wrote in *Wisden*, and Charles' camera offers some confirmation of this. In particular, the veteran Bruce Mitchell took almost six hours to score 120, and the filmed evidence is of a batsman with little back-lift, scoring his runs with painstaking care.

Charles, meanwhile, spent the rest day away from it all, enjoying a freer life than post-war England allowed. 'I borrowed an enormous American car,' he wrote home to Barbara, 'and went for a long spin in the country all by myself. Quite an experience driving a car where one never changed gear. And it could do 100 (not that I did).'

There then followed a month of provincial matches, in which Charles finally found some form. At Port Elizabeth, against Eastern Province, he opened the innings and hit 116 and 57, and this had the reporters enjoying once more the schoolmaster jokes. Frank Rostron in the *Daily Express* talked of 'a beano which his pupils at Bromsgrove would have enjoyed,' while Alex Bannister in the *Daily Mail* was able to cable back: 'Now his half-tour report will read: "After a bad start, showing his best form. His latest innings was most satisfactory, and it is to be hoped that the improvement will be maintained."'

The runs had come too late to give Charles any chance of breaking into the Test side, where all the batsmen were in good form, and once more he was a cameraman for the fourth Test at Johannesburg, a third drawn match, and the final Test at Port Elizabeth, where the game burst into life when South Africa's captain Dudley Nourse set England to score 172 in just 95 minutes. Gamely England went for the runs and, with seven wickets down, they still wanted 19 for victory. But the often cautious Jack Crapp opened his shoulders and, with ten runs in three balls, won the match with just a minute to spare, transporting John Arlott once more to the heights of celebration:

PALMER IS IN TEST PICTURE

From CRAWFORD WHITE

PORT ELIZABETH, Sunday.

REACTING from the severity of recent concentration of Test play and intensive travel, M.C.C. have gone into this game in festival spirit, and the Eastern Province side, captained by ex-Lancashire League professional Sid Hird, look easy meat.

George Mann, however, does not intend to waste any opportunities, and tomorrow he will be working his bowlers—especially left-hander Jack Young—with the fourth Test (a month ahead) in mind.

Compton gets another

Most pleasing thing in Saturday's play was the excellent first century by Charlie Palmer, hitherto the victim of bad luck. He was timing the ball so well that he cannot be ruled out of the next Test possibles.

Alan Watkins and Cliff Gladwin also made their highest scores to date and Compton, with an ease which made the bowling look juvenile, came along with the century which seemed inevitable from the moment he hit his first ball. This was his sixth hundred of the tour.

M.C.C.

R T Simpson b Hicks	40
C Palmer b Dutoit	116
J Crapp b Murray	3
D Compton c Jordan b Hird	103
A Watkins b Young	83
F G Mann c Burrell b Dutoit	22
M Tremlett b Young	1
S C Griffith, b Dutoit	0
C Gladwin not out	52
D Wright b Hicks	6
J Young not out	11
Extras (b 6, nb 1, lb 1)	8
Total (9 wkts)	450

Fall of Wickets: 1-97, 2-104, 3-219, 4-287, 5-308, 6-342, 7-343, 8-417, 9-434.

Bowling to Date: Hicks 20-0-93-2, Dutoit 19-1-74-3, Young 25-1-85-2, Hird 15-2-49-1, Murray 12-0-70-1, Jordan 4-0-43-0, Burrell 4-0-23-0.

> I never thought this could happen twice in a series. England win by three wickets. It's an incredible finish. They've made 170 runs in ninety minutes. At a rate of almost 120 an hour. On a turner, with Athol Rowan and Tufty Mann, believe me, bowling very well indeed.

For the England captain George Mann, the tour had been a triumph. He was a selfless and inspiring skipper, and his century in the first innings of the final Test was a popular one. And his own triumphant tour had the best of endings when, on the boat home, he met the woman who would become his wife.

The tourists had travelled more than 10,000 miles around South Africa. They had enjoyed outstanding success on the field and made countless friends off it. "We had fun," Charles emphasises, and his film shows the team enjoying their introduction to tribal dances, as well as playing some golf, with trilby hats the order of the day on the tee.

'For the last week,' he wrote to Barbara, 'I've had the golf bug. Sometimes I hit a smacker and it goes many a mile down the fairway and then, just when I begin to smile, it decides to turn left or right and I have to plough through a wood or some undergrowth to find the ball. And then do I tell that perishing bit of white mischief what I think of it!'

With fellow novice Reg Simpson, Charles bought an instructional book. "It was called 'The nine bad shots of golf'. Well it wasn't nine; we thought it was more like a hundred and nine."

"I remember being in the bedroom with this book," Reg says, "and Charles over the other side with the clubs. And I looked at him and said, 'That club wants to be further round that way.' And we learnt to grip the club properly."

"Then we played at Port Elizabeth in a little rabbits' competition for beginners. And on one occasion Charlie hit the ball off the tee into some rough about a hundred and fifty yards away. When we got there, Charlie went diving into the long grass, looking for his ball. No sign of it. But his caddy wouldn't join him to look for it. We said, 'Why don't you come and look? You're supposed to be a caddie.' He said, 'Mambas, mambas down there.' Apparently they knew that mambas nested in this area, and Charlie had gone diving in. But the old caddie wasn't risking it."

Married a fortnight before setting sail, Reg Simpson admits to moments when he felt homesick and to disappointment that he played in only the first Test, but Charles helped to keep his spirits up. "You couldn't have wished to have a nicer fellow to be with. He was so relaxed and never upset at not being selected or anything like that. He kept me sane, I think."

In their travels they all enjoyed the rich variety of the landscape, from the majesty of Victoria Falls to the breathtaking panoramic views from the top of Table Mountain. Most of their longer journeys were by train and none was more memorable than the one they undertook after the final Test, travelling along the Garden Route from Port Elizabeth to Cape Town in their own observation car at the back of the train. Here a piano was laid on and in their private carriage, with Charles or Jack Young at the keyboard, the team could celebrate in song without risk of disturbing other passengers.

It was their fourth visit to Cape Town and the lovely Newlands ground, this time to play the Combined Universities. It was a match of little serious consequence, attracting few spectators, though Charles has not forgotten one of them, whom he met while he was fielding at deep square leg – under the famous old oak trees, "now desecrated by the concrete jungle."

"I was on the boundary, not taking much notice of the game because the interest had faded away, and I happened to be stationed by the captain at a place which was only a few yards away from one spectator – and she was really very nice indeed. And I'm afraid my attention wandered from the game to the spectator, and we had a nice little chat. Then suddenly she said, 'Oh, the captain's waving. He wants you.' And there was George Mann semaphoring to me to move away from this girl. But he only moved me about two yards, just to make the point to get me away from this girl."

Charles recalls the same match for a press box prank. "Frank Rostron, who wrote for the *Daily Express*, decided that it wasn't really a match worth bothering about, so he went to play golf and deputed one of his colleagues to tell him what had happened so he could dash something off when he got back. Well, they ganged up against him and they gave him the wrong information. And this went flying over the ether to England. I don't think I've ever seen a man so angry!"

This was South Africa before the scourge of apartheid had taken hold as a declared political policy, and one of the team's most memorable moments was meeting Field Marshal Smuts at Parliament House. He had recently been succeeded as prime minister by Dr Daniel Malan, several of whose Afrikaans-based Nationalist party had supported Hitler during the War and who would soon set the country on the road to international isolation. When the players met Smuts, he was about to go off to a garden party to celebrate Malan's election. "I'd rather be with you boys," he said before departing.

Though there was not yet any legislation enforcing the apartheid code, the team nevertheless were almost exclusively in the company of white people, and most of them were English rather than Afrikaner by descent. "Apartheid hadn't come into being really," Charles says. "It certainly didn't impinge on cricket, as we saw it as tourists. But everything was dictated by the whites and, if you were a black person, you were expected to get off the pavement if a white person was walking down the street."

Thirty years later, with South Africa excluded from world cricket, Charles would return as Chairman of the International Cricket Conference to hear their pleas for reinstatement. And the happy memories of his five months there with George Mann's team would still be with him.

They had escaped from a winter of austerity and, though clothes rationing in Britain ended three days before they started home on the *Stirling Castle*, their well-being as tourists owed little to the finances of MCC. 'We've been given another £75 by the South African Cricket Association,' he wrote to Barbara, 'and very useful too – because otherwise I should have been about £35 overspent by the time we get home.'

CHAPTER 7

LEICESTERSHIRE GET THEIR MAN

"They've got no money, they've got no side, they've got no ground, they've been bottom of the chart for the last couple of years. What are you going there for?" Brigadier Mike Green's question was forthright as Charles weighed up an offer to join Leicestershire as captain and Secretary. Mike Green, tour manager in South Africa, was his county Secretary at Worcester, and Charles had come to respect his judgment. Yet Green's counsel did not deter him from making the decision that would change the direction of his life and set him on a course that would take him to the major offices in the game.

Charles had begun to wonder if he would ever leave the comfortable situation of a public school common room. He had enjoyed his time at Bromsgrove, but he had a yearning for wider pastures. "There were no ulcers around in a public school in those days, but it was a slightly introverted society that you lived in, inevitably so. You were there seven days a week with each other and I think I'd just got the feeling that I'd been out in the world for six years and I wanted to see what was going on in the world now, which I couldn't do staying within the four walls of Bromsgrove School."

After a successful summer in 1949, Charles fancied a job that would give him the chance to play more cricket, perhaps combining playing with administrative and management duties as Wilf Wooller at Glamorgan and Desmond Eagar at Hampshire were doing. "One day in the masters' common room, a colleague told me that he'd spotted an advert that he thought might interest me. Somerset County Cricket Club were looking for a Captain/ Secretary."

His pupil Nigel Sisson still retains the diary in which he recorded the progress of Charles' application:

> I saw in the paper that out of 20 applicants for the office of Secretary of Somerset next summer Charlie has been short-listed among others. The job is offered at £750 a year, but he has always scorned a pro's life when he talks to us. However, if he wants to get anywhere, that is the way he must go. But I do hope he doesn't go as he is a terribly good chap to have as coach and he is, of course, a great asset to the cricket of the school.

The retiring Secretary of Somerset was Brigadier E.H. Lancaster, who – according to Peter Roebuck's history of the county club – 'was worn down by years of battles with committees and members. Life had been simpler in the Army, with its authoritarian structure. It had been easier at Somerset, too, when it was more or less a private club run by a handful of distinguished locals. Now it was a members' club, with a tangled web of committees and interested parties.'

"I had an extraordinary interview," Charles remembers. "There were 43 people there – or so I was told. I neither had the time nor the inclination to count them. But there seemed no way that I could work with them."

Somerset appointed as Secretary the son of Lancaster's predecessor, and he had had enough at the end of one summer. Meanwhile they continued to look to amateur captains, eight in the first ten years after the war, and from 1952 to 1955 they were bottom of the championship table every year.

Charles, meanwhile, had lost his enthusiasm for such a career move. "After the Somerset fiasco I thought if that's cricket I'll return to my study." So when a similar post – captain and Secretary at Leicestershire – was drawn to his attention, he did not apply.

Before placing their advertisement, Leicestershire had already suffered the disappointment of losing a candidate from the Newcastle area to whom they had offered the job. This prompted the committee to consider other avenues, and the minutes of 30th November 1949 record that 'a letter had been sent to Somersetshire, asking them if, when they had made their final choice for Secretary etc., they would hand on to us the names of any other applicants who might be suitable for our post."

Perhaps it was from Somerset that Frank Smith, then Chairman of the county club, first learnt that Charles had shown an interest in a full-time post in cricket. He only knew of him from afar, but he clearly believed that he was just the man for Leicestershire.

Frank Smith had once driven a milk float, but in 1915 he had bought into the then small dairy firm of Kirby and West and he had developed it into a business that had made him a millionaire. The determination that had built the dairy empire was now being applied to the cause of Leicestershire County Cricket Club. Frank Smith was a man with a mission – to get Palmer – and his telephone calls were not easily rebuffed by Charles.

"Charles was playing hockey at Worcester," says Barbara, "and Frank Smith rang. He said, 'What time will your husband get back?' Well, in those days we didn't have a car so I said, 'I really haven't the remotest idea. He relies on other people for lifts, and he might be quite late.' And he said, 'It doesn't matter how late it is. Would you please get him to ring me when he comes home?' That was Frank Smith, no messing about. He said, 'Whatever you do, and I don't mind how late it is, twelve o'clock, one o'clock, two o'clock, three o'clock, make sure he rings me when he comes home.' So I did."

Eventually Charles and Barbara, who was heavily pregnant with their second child, were persuaded to go over to Leicester where the Chairman showed them areas of the city where they might buy a house – and it was all very different from what Charles was expecting. "I thought, 'I'm going into a little office with a tall stool, writing with a pen and ink.' Then the first thing we did when we got out at the station was to get into a very large Daimler. Suddenly we found we were talking to a man of consequence."

The cricket club might have been impoverished, but the city was not. "I think at the time that it was the second most prosperous city in Europe," Barbara says. "With all the hosiery manufacturers, supplying Marks and

Spencers and places like that. I went to one function, and I was introduced to five millionaires. They were two a penny in Leicester."

Frank Smith persuaded Charles at least to apply for the advertised post. So there was an upbeat note in the minutes of the club's next meeting: 'The Chairman reported that several applications of mediocre calibre had been received. The only letter of real interest was from CH Palmer.'

Charles had been attracted by Frank Smith's dedication – "He was a man of steel" – and this time there was a panel of only three for the formal interview, Smith being accompanied by CH Gimson and AS Broughton. If Charles was still wavering, he was soon won over by Chris Gimson, a charismatic bachelor who had played a few matches for the county in 1921 and who had now retired from a distinguished career in the Indian Civil Service. After talking it over with Barbara, Charles decided to take the plunge. "It was a three-year contract at the start and inevitably rather more money than I was getting as a schoolmaster. So I came to Leicester."

The grandson of Frank Smith – Brian – has himself played a major role in the club, serving as President in the 1990s, and, though only a boy at the time, he recalls his grandfather's excitement at the prospect of capturing the Worcestershire schoolmaster as a playing secretary. With Eagar and Wooller, and later Trevor Bailey at Essex, this combination of roles was becoming a common device for retaining amateurs in the first-class game.

Barbara and Charles, with Mr & Mrs Frank Smith

Charles would soon come to know the Smith family well, and Brian Smith recalls how, after his grandmother had died in 1953, his grandfather had gone out to the West Indies to watch England on the tour which Charles managed. "Charles was ever so good," says Brian. "He looked after my grandfather, and I remember going to collect him when they came into Bristol. He was a tremendous help to the family."

When his appointment as Secretary was announced in February 1950, Charles knew that he was facing a challenge. The side had hit rock bottom, ending the 1949 season at the foot of the table, and a few enquiries would soon establish that the club was run on a shoestring. For good measure the coach, Fred Root, had also resigned, and for the 1950 season there were insufficient funds to replace him.

It was fortunate for the county that, at a time when players were not permitted to flit from one county to the next in search of a better deal, MCC approved a special registration that enabled Charles to play in this first summer before he had acquired a residential qualification. Thus he was able to take up the reins of captaincy at the start of the season.

One who remembers the early post-war years before Charles' arrival is Vic Munden, who had a trial in 1946 as a local 18-year-old with aspirations to bowl fast and who found himself taken on as a slow bowler. "They said, 'You're not big enough, you're not broad enough, so if you come on the staff it's on condition you bowl slow.'" But, before he could sign, his call-up papers arrived and his only appearances in that first summer after the war were as Aircraftsman Munden, specially released from his camp. Leicestershire were so short that he played in four matches, the highlight of his summer being when he came out to bat at number eleven against the champions Yorkshire. Leicestershire were nine wickets down, on the verge of defeat, and there were still 35 minutes to be played. The 13-year-old MJK Smith, later to captain England, was there that day. "I can remember him holding out," he says. "Yorkshire didn't win the game." Or, as *Wisden* put it, 'Munden rose to the occasion and played out the last over coolly.'

Another survivor of that first post-war season and its occasionally desperate measures to find eleven players to take the field is John Josephs, Chairman of the club in the 1990s. At the time a 22-year-old amateur with few credentials for the first-class game, he played his third county match at Bristol, where some who came to watch would have known him from his schooldays at nearby Clifton. "I remember facing Tom Goddard, and I wondered how I was ever going to get off the mark." In the first innings he failed to do so.

Walter Hammond made 113 when Gloucestershire batted. He was already well set when young Josephs was brought on to bowl his left-arm spinners. "I could see a little grin on his face. He hit me for four through the covers and I remember Reg Sinfield, who was my coach at Clifton, saying to me that if a chap starts hitting you through the covers, bowl it wider. 'Throw it up, bowl it wider and wider.' So that's what's I did. And a broader grin came on

Hammond's face, and the ball bounced back off the railings into the centre almost!"

Five years later, playing the eighth of his ten games for Leicestershire, John took his only first-class wicket when a ball that had bounced twice was spooned to cover by Gilbert Parkhouse. "The *Sunday Graphic* called it the worst ball bowled since the First World War," he recalls, quietly relishing the thought that this is not a newspaper that has survived into the modern era.

Joining the staff full-time in 1948, Vic Munden remembers the Secretary of the day: "GOJ Elliott, we used to call him 'Goje' for short. He was a stout man, a broad fellow. He had GOJE right across his sweater in big letters. He used to skipper the Club and Ground side. It was nearly all amateurs. I think we only had about twelve pros, possibly thirteen."

There was little in the way of support staff, as far as Vic can recall, though the name of Tony Morley springs to mind. "He was the so-called masseur. He was only a rub man really. He didn't know what he was doing. He was there about four years. He just used to get you on the table for something to do, I think."

For Charles' predecessor there had been no cash to spare. The only reserves comprised the compensation received when the Aylestone Road ground, the pre-war home, had been lost to first-class cricket when an electricity generating station was extended across the practice ground. The county had returned to Grace Road, its home at the turn of the century, still with its 1889 pavilion, but the move had only been made possible through a generous concession of the Leicester Education Committee, whose own requirements limited the number of matches that could be played there.

Vic Munden, who remembers the ground from his time as a pupil at the City Boys' School, recalls returning to it as a first-class cricketer. "There was a square in the middle, and there were four football pitches all the way round it. So sometimes it was really rough in the outfield. And we also had an Education groundsman, who was only more or less a grass cutter. May be a bit unfair to him, but that's what he was."

The county's minutes from April 1950 record the hope that they might be enabled to re-engage 'a groundsman who used to be with us.' But there was no joy for the committee because 'the Education Committee had viewed the suggestion with disfavour, and the matter was therefore dropped.' So the players of the early post-war years soldiered on, a couple of them speaking of the fear that they might have their teeth knocked out if called upon to field a ball near one of the goal areas in the outfield.

"The whole pavilion was terrible," says Vic. "We were a bit of a ragtail club before Charles came. We'd got no money, nothing to spend on things like that. It must have been years and years old because, when I was in the second team, the dressing rooms for the second teams were nearly underground."

Vic remembers that parsimony stretched to the team's attire. "I was looking at the old photographs for '48 and I think everyone had got a different sweater on because there were no club sweaters. There was a blazer but that was held over from before the war. It was green with red braid and a fox on the pocket. I don't think the club had got enough money for sweaters and blazers. In about '51 or '52 we all went down to Simpsons in London to be measured for blazers: bottle green blazers with a leaping fox on the pocket."

For the first three seasons after the war Leicestershire had not managed to find an amateur who might take on the captaincy of the first team; so it had fallen to the senior professional, Les Berry, who had first played for the county in 1924, to take on the mantle. Finishing 11th, 14th and 11th was all that a county of such modest resources could expect whoever was in charge; but to have an amateur as captain still remained Leicestershire's dream.

In those early post-war seasons all the counties wanted amateur captains, and sometimes there was a hint of desperation in their searches.

"I played for Notts in the summer of '46," Reg Simpson recalls. "Then, round about Christmas, I had a phone call from the father of a friend of an Old Nottinghamian who I was playing rugger with. 'Would you like to skipper Northants?' he said. 'What is all this about?' I said. 'Is it a joke?' 'No,' he said. 'I'm perfectly serious. If you say yes, I'll fix up a meeting with the committee.' I was still in the police force that winter, but I said, 'Fair enough' and I went over to Northampton and eventually I was told, 'We'll take you on.'"

News of the offer reached the ears of the Notts Chairman. "He said, 'No way is Simpson going to Northants.' So we had a bit of squabbling over terms, and eventually I signed up for Notts." A job was found for him with Gunn and Moore, and Reg was able to play full-time cricket, as an amateur, for the next 14 years, captaining the county from 1951 to 1960.

Meanwhile, Northamptonshire recruited Arthur Childs-Clarke, who had played ten times as an amateur for Middlesex between 1923 and 1934. *Wisden* described his batting as 'gallant', but his captaincy was unable to lift the county off the foot of the championship table.

For the 1949 season Leicestershire turned to SJ Symington. A member of the local corset-making family, he was a serving officer in the Army. In 1949, at the age of 22, he was able to take half a season's leave and this was enough for Leicestershire to appoint him captain. "A larger than life character" is how Lol Spence, then a 17-year-old recruit, remembers him. "Very bubbly, he laughed a lot. But his cricketing abilities were limited."

He took the new ball with little success, and Somerset's opener Eric Hill recalls an early game when both he and his dashing partner Harold Gimblett were dismissed by the young Symington. "We both played careless shots, and Gimmo was furious. I said, 'Keep your hair on' but, as soon as he went in the second time, he started bashing as though there was no tomorrow. And after two or three overs, this poor bloke Symington's stood in the middle of the pitch. 'If this is first-class cricket,' he's muttering, 'I've bloody well had it.' And Gimmo looked up and said, 'You want to thank your lucky stars that Charlie Barnett's given up the game.'"

"How he bowled, I don't know," says Vic Munden. "He was a big porky lad, about 17 stone. He'd hardly played until he skippered the side, and looking back he hadn't much of a clue. I mean, I didn't know much then, but he used to go to the older pros, Maurice Tompkin and Les Berry. Les always used to travel with him because Symington wanted to pick his brains on what was going on.

"I know Les used to be frightened to death when he drove with him. When he was about 40 or 50 yards from the green light, it was 'If it changes now, I'm going through.' Another time it was red and he came crashing up to it. 'I'm going through whether they change or not!' And Les used to lean forward and turn the ignition off."

So this was the man who had taken charge for most of the season before Charles arrived at Grace Road. Had there been handover notes? "I never met him. I thought I'd met him when Leicestershire had come to Worcester in 1949. I kept on calling him Mr Symington, or Stuart or whatever his name was, only to find out at the end of the game that it wasn't Symington at all. It was a different chap altogether."

This, it transpired, was another amateur drafted in for the last eight matches after Symington had returned to military duties. Gwynn Evans had won a Blue at Oxford in 1939 and played seven games for Glamorgan later that summer; but these credentials were not apparent when he first appeared in the Leicester dressing room. "He was only a club cricketer," Vic Munden recalls, "but he skippered us for some reason and he made a mess of it as well.

"The first day he came in and he gave us all a sheet of paper. 'This is where you will field for Jim Sperry, this is where you will field for Jack Walsh, this is where you will field for Vic Jackson.' The wicket-keeper was Paddy Corrall and he stuttered a bit when he got excited and he said, ''I'm n-not l-looking at that.' Vic Jackson said 'Why not? You've got to.' He said 'I kn-know where I'm s-standing.'

"Then we played Sussex, and they'd got about six left-handers and the skipper had only made the sheets out for right-handers. I think he gave up after that."

Vic Munden recalls another moment of ineptitude from the match against Sussex: "Walshy was bowling when George Cox came in, and he wanted to get away from Walshy until he got set. Well, he hit Jack down the ground and Evans chased it for two. Well, it should have been two. But he picked the ball up and, instead of throwing it, he came in tossing it from hand to hand and he thought George wasn't going again. But George wanted to get away from Walshy, and he got the third run. I daren't tell you what Walshy said about throwing it in!"

Whatever the club might have hoped to gain from the tenure of Symington and Evans, Leicestershire had sunk to the bottom of the table, their three victories only half the number recorded by the team immediately above them. It was the nadir of their playing fortunes.

Whatever the shortcomings of the captains, however, there was in the side a core of useful performers, whom Charles would soon come to respect and like. "We'd got a decent side," he says, "but they needed pulling together. And they were all very anxious to do well."

Vic Munden remembers the air of anticipation before Charles arrived. "Billy Burrell, one of the committee members, said, 'From now on it should be all right. If we get this fellow, we shall be all right.'"

There were a few gaps to be plugged, but Charles himself would bring extra solidity to the batting and a few steadying overs of seam. But before he could think too hard about the playing side, there was a bigger job to be done if the club was to survive. "I looked at the balance sheet and I said, 'Palmer, you may stay here for two years or three years, but that's about your limit before the money runs out.'"

In the post-war world, where few men could afford to play as genuine amateurs, a certain 'shamateurism' was developing. Back in 1948 the previous Secretary had reported to the committee that he had been approached by one of the county's top order batsmen, Frank Prentice, a well-established professional nearing the end of his career. The minutes record that 'Prentice had been on the telephone to him and that he possibly would like to play as an amateur in 1948.' They then state that 'he also required to be paid expenses which would bring him in as much as if he were to play as a professional.' His offer was turned down.

For Charles, however, the county was prepared to pay good money. He started on £1,000 a year, a figure that was planned to rise to £1,200. He also received £2 a week for his general expenses and a mileage allowance for his car, and for £78 a year the club housed him. This financial package compared with a basic salary of £450 for established professionals like Berry, Tompkin, Lester and Jackson.

But Leicestershire were not looking for a good cricketer with phantom responsibilities in the office. His off-the-field duties enabled Charles to continue playing with his initials ahead of his name, but the post of Secretary was no comfortable nine to five job, let alone a sinecure. He had minimal paid help in the office and, in the winter, he put in long evenings around the county as he became consumed by one passionate desire: to restore the financial fortunes of the club.

CHAPTER 8

THE CINDERELLA COUNTY

"I went to fifty dinners in the first year to spread the gospel," Charles says. "Always chicken and salad. It was getting to know the people that was the important thing. But I enjoyed it, and I made plenty of friends that way."

Some of the dinners were white tie affairs, and Barbara would accompany her husband. "I had to have gloves," she says. "Oh yes, you had to dress up a bit. We'd got out of that habit during the war, and I thought it was jolly nice. I miss it these days."

Invariably Charles would be speaking. For Barbara's father it had always been an ordeal to speak in public. "He was a successful architect and a most self-confident bloke, but he was terrified of making a speech. He used to practise out loud at home, perhaps in his bedroom. So, to me, making a speech was the most ghastly ordeal any man could go through.

"So, when I came to Leicester and heard Charles speak for the first time, I was curdling inside. And out it came as natural as anything you've ever heard in your life. I couldn't get over it. So I didn't have to get in a state like my poor old mum used to do. It was a revelation to me. And it still is."

Charles wasted no time in tackling the financial problems at Leicester, but he could not do it alone and he looks back with gratitude to those who helped him in the gargantuan task he faced. "There were some marvellous people on the committee who had got the interests of the club at heart. It was not self-aggrandisement as far as they were concerned. And I thoroughly enjoyed working with them."

The committee was not as large as at most of the counties, and there was a down-to-earth supportiveness for Charles as he attempted to tackle the problems of the struggling club. "Frank Smith always used to tell me that the solution of one problem invariably created another. And there was another man on the committee, an avuncular chap, who – whenever failure rapidly followed success – would say, 'Don't forget, my boy,' – I was 31 at the time! – 'The Lord doesn't give with both hands.'"

Frank Smith proved a staunch and determined chairman with whom to work, but Charles also singles out Chris Gimson. This was the man to whom he would always turn when he wanted an objective answer to a difficult question. He would later become Vice-Chairman when Charles himself assumed the chairmanship of the county club.

"He really was marvellous, but very much the old-fashioned type. I remember him inviting us to dinner. He'd got one of these very large houses, and we went there and he did everything right. There was a panelled dining room with a lavatory off it and all that sort of thing. We had dined and had a very good meal and then came the time to have a glass of port. And he stood up and took Barbara by the hand and escorted her to the drawing room, sat her down there and came back. She sat all alone like a bloody prune in this vast drawing room."

Gimson shared the Palmers' love of music, and they would go to concerts together. One day he also shared with Charles his secret in learning to appreciate a difficult piece. "Late Beethoven quartets, that sort of thing, he said, 'When I'm by myself I put the record on and I'll play it and play it and play it without listening to it. Then one day I'll say, now I'll listen to it.' And, of course, he knew it. It's a very good way of learning something that you don't want to learn."

Charles was soon looking for Gimson's support for a radical measure he was planning in relation to the club's finances. "I was still in close contact with Worcestershire, and it was about this time that they started running a football pool. It had originally started at a church in Hereford. A shilling a week. So you tapped the masses rather than the big benefactors. I came to Leicester thinking, 'That's a damn good idea to make some money.' So I tried to sell it to the committee."

Charles took the trouble to talk individually with each committee member to ensure the safe passage of his scheme, and he won their support. "It kept us out of penury. Fortunately there were an enormous number of people willing to help. It needs an army of people to run that sort of thing properly."

John Josephs, who had a spell on the committee as a very young man and who later captained the Second Eleven, remembers lending a hand with the venture, which was run by a cricket-mad market clothing dealer, Bill Butler. His partner in the enterprise was Sid Norman, and together they also spent evenings as a sort of music hall act. "Every Saturday morning I used to go down there to collect in all this money that people brought in. And it raised an enormous amount.

"We tried to get permission from the Chief Constable to run it. And he said 'I can't give you permission to run it. But you haven't asked me, and I don't know anything about it.' So we took that as being OK. And after a week or two he won the first prize, and he rang up and said, 'For God's sake don't publicise this.'"

So, as Charles learnt what it was to dine out every evening on chicken and salad and John Josephs gave up his Saturday mornings to the cause, the cash flowed in. In two and a half years a club with assets of only £5,000 found that it had raised an extra £22,000.

An early priority for spending was on improvements to the ground. "It progressed so well that we were able to get seats without splinters," Charles quips, remembering the riposte from Tom Graveney when it had been jokingly suggested that he might care to switch counties: "I daren't. I'm afraid of getting all the splinters from the dressing room benches in my bottom."

Money alone could not solve Leicestershire's ground difficulties. "The Director of Education was most co-operative, but they could only allow us to play at Grace Road for four matches in term time. That's why we took the matches all around the county, like Essex used to do. It was grossly uneconomical, but that's what we had to do. And there wasn't a ground that was well equipped. Even Grace Road was only a school sports ground, with no facilities whatsoever." Or, as the Essex batsman Dickie Dodds wrote, 'Grace Road was a ground that needed all the grace it could get.'

Ground developments. The stand at Aylestone Road has been erected at Grace Road.

The Town Ground at Coalville, the Bath Ground at Ashby-de-la-Zouch and Park Road, Loughborough were the other venues where Leicester hosted matches in Charles' first season. The next year Hinckley was added, replacing Coalville's Town Ground, which was dropped, never to return, after just one county match. In 1953 the Loughborough matches moved from Park Road to the Brush Ground. Then in 1957 problems at Grace Road necessitated a brief return to Aylestone Road, where two matches were played in the shadow of the cooling towers. Later that year there was a revival of first-class cricket at Coalville, but this time it took place at the Snibston Colliery Ground, with a slag heap alongside. For Jack Birkenshaw of a later generation, this was the grimmest ground in England. "If the wind blew the wrong way, you were in trouble."

Charles has a different perspective. "When we played at Coalville first, it was at the Town Ground, not at Snibston, and it was absolutely dreadful," he says. "And who should we have to entertain there but Warwickshire with all their loads of lolly? Compared with that, the Snibston Colliery ground was a vast improvement. It was like the difference between light and dark. Snibston wasn't that great, but you didn't have to apologise every five minutes, like you did at the Town Ground. That absolutely was the bottom of the pile."

Strangely, for all his negative memories of the Town Ground at Coalville, Charles fails to mention that it was here in June of his first summer as Leicestershire's captain that he scored his first century for the club – with a 'faultless' 143 against a Warwickshire bowling attack that the following summer would win them the County Championship.

In 1954 Tony Diment became Charles' assistant in the office, later succeeding him as Secretary. He also played some matches for the county when he could be spared; but his early season priority was negotiating with each of the outground clubs to agree arrangements for the matches. "We didn't have stands in those days; we had a ring of seats round the ground. We'd have contractors taking 50 or 60 benches out to Hinckley in furniture vans, and scoreboards and various tents. It was pretty basic really, but it all had to be coordinated."

Sight screens were another problem, as the young fast bowler Terry Spencer remembers: "Some of the canvas ones were not very good. Today they cover the whole thing, round the wicket or whatever you're bowling, but in those days you had to move them every other ball. You had to have a couple of boys at each end to watch the game and shift them."

The pitches, Tony Diment feels, were at least of good club standard, "but they possibly broke up a bit quicker than they did at Grace Road. A lot of pride came into this and the people whose ground we were going to, made a big effort to make sure that the wicket was good."

In the memory of Jeff Goodwin, another young fast bowler at this time, the quality of some of the pitches could be more variable. His first season saw Leicestershire beaten by an innings by Kent on the Park Road Ground at Loughborough. "It was like a ploughed field, and Doug Wright bowled us out twice. When he was on form, he used to turn the ball viciously."

Of the out-grounds Ashby-de-la-Zouch was Charles' favourite. "It was a very pleasant country ground. There was a railway right behind, but that didn't make any difference. The trains didn't go that often. There was a lovely hotel, where we had a jolly good lunch."

Jeff Goodwin is another who looks back fondly to matches at Ashby. He wasn't too keen on the "antiquated pavilion", which consisted of a couple of converted railway carriages, but his eyes lit up at the memory of trooping off for lunch at the Royal Hotel in 'The Palisade'. "Very nice it was too!"

'The Ashby-de-la-Zouch ground was as improbable as its name,' Dickie Dodds wrote: 'We stayed at the Royal, changed for the game in our bedrooms, and then walked through the gardens of the hotel and entered the rural cricket ground through a private gate. It was like country house cricket.'

Charles' first visit to Ashby was as a Worcestershire player. "It rained cats and dogs," he recalls, "and the Worcestershire players in particular, led by Allan White, sank pint after pint because we all thought, 'There'll be no play today.' Well, the sun came out with tropical intensity, and we were out there by about three or three thirty. And everybody wanted a pee. When the first wicket fell, we all rushed off. The pavilion was about the size of this room, with two little loos at the end. It took us ages to start the game again."

The traditional fixture at Ashby was against Derbyshire, and Jeff Goodwin remembers that "the miners used to come from miles around. But one year we played Surrey. There was one man and his dog there. We never saw one miner turn up when we played them! Absolutely killed it."

When Terry Spencer joined the team in 1952, facilities at Grace Road were little better than at the outgrounds. "The pavilion when I started, God it was dreadful. We had the dressing rooms in this wooden shack or whatever you like to call it, right down in the basement below eye level, and to get down you had to walk down these stairs that were all wooden and had been spiked over the years. You used to get splinters in your feet; everything was wooden, and nails showing through the floorboards. But it didn't bother us so much in those days, as it would today with all the health and safety people. We just got on with it."

"The committee room was a joke," says Charles. In the winter committee meetings would take place in the county's city centre offices at Spencer Chambers, but if they gathered at the ground it was in a tiny room around a couple of furniture removers' packing cases. Not that committee members' comfort was much better catered for at Spencer Chambers, a minute from a meeting in February 1954 recording that 'in view of the instability of the seats in the committee room, it was agreed to purchase eighteen new chairs.'

There was plenty for long-suffering spectators to complain about at Grace Road as well, but Tony Diment worked out how to keep them content: "I always found that you got the moans from people not about whether there were enough seats and that they had to stand for five hours to watch a game, but whether the loos had enough lavatory paper. That's when somebody would come barging in very indignantly: 'There's no loo paper.' It was the little things that mattered."

John Josephs remembers the measures that needed to be taken to accommodate spectators for the match with the Australians in 1953. "The Meet stand, or most of it, was transferred from the Aylestone Road ground, and we brought a lot of seats that went on the top. And we thought we'd got it ready the day before the match but, when the police came to inspect it all, they decided that it was not at all safe. And we had to bolt down every single seat. All night we were bolting down seats."

Perhaps the Grace Road square produced pitches that lasted longer than at Hinckley or Loughborough, but there were still days when the bowlers were too much on top. One instance sticks in Vic Munden's mind. "I think it's the only time I saw Charles get really annoyed. We were playing Surrey. Lockie and Laker were playing, and I think we bowled them out and then we went in and it was like a dust bowl. We'd got no chance. We got bowled out on the third day. I've forgotten how Charles got out but, before he'd taken his pads off, he went down to the groundsman's shed and sorted him out."

The players had foreseen the trouble before the match started, as Vic Munden relates. "We were practising and I was with Bill Ashdown, the coach, and I said, 'Look at him, Bill.' And the groundsman was shovelling marl on, and this was the day before the match. There were clouds of dust; it was like a desert. Well, he watered it in, but of course next day it was all loose so the top went."

These were the problems the county faced in laying on cricket matches for the public but, when Charles arrived, he also had to lift the team from its failures of the previous summer. "They'd got some good players, but they were under-achieving, as they say now," he says. His senior professional was the 44-year-old Les Berry, the highest run-scorer in the county's history, and he was still a good enough batsman to score more than 1,600 runs that summer. "He tried very hard, but he was getting to the end of his cricket enjoyment. It was amusing to watch him in the field. You could see his legs running, but his body wasn't moving."

Berry's role as leading run-maker had passed to Maurice Tompkin, a fine straight-driver of the ball. "He was one of the nicest guys I've ever met on a cricket field," says Charles of the man who became his senior professional in 1955. "And with Maurice around, I never had any problems in the dressing room. Any problem had been sorted out before it came to me. And he did it in such a nice way. A gentleman in every sense of the word, and a damn good cricketer too."

The old Leicestershire players have been generous in their recollections of the colleagues alongside whom they played, but all have made it clear that Tompkin was a man apart. "I don't think anyone ever said a bad word about Maurice," says Vic Munden. Over the next six seasons Charles and Tompkin would be unchallenged as the county's top pair in the batting averages. Then, in 1956, at the height of his powers Tompkin would have a summer wracked by ill health and die within weeks of the season ending.

Gerry Lester was another established player who helped Charles to mould a stronger side. "A great trier," says Charles, and Vic Munden echoes the same sentiment, recalling him as a brave batsman in a side where one or two did not relish the quicker bowling. "Gerry would stand it. A broad pigeon-chested lad, he said, 'When they hit you, you don't have to show when you're hurt.' He'd just chest it away."

One who was less keen on facing the pace merchants was the Australian Vic Jackson. "But he'd murder the others when he was in, especially the spinners," says Vic Munden. "He could play the spinners in his sleep," Jeff Goodwin agrees.

Vic Jackson was also a key member of the attack with his off-spinners, and his bowling complemented his fellow Australian Jack Walsh, the most feared of Leicestershire's bowlers of the early post-war years. "Jack Walsh was the best left-arm spinner I've ever seen, with his chinaman," says Charles. "With young Munden bowling left-arm tweakers, it was quite a balanced spin attack."

The main weakness was the pace bowling. The long-serving left-armer Jim Sperry was 40 when Charles arrived at the club, and the previous year it had been the short-term captains who had usually shared the new ball with him. Tall but slightly built, his physique was immortalised for Vic Munden by Paddy Corrall when he saw Sperry stripping for action in the dressing room: "Cor, Jim, you're like a greyhound that's been sandpapered down!" "Jim was a really good solid, old professional of the old type," says Charles. "If you put him on into a howling gale, he'd bowl into a howling gale."

For that first year the attack was strengthened by the presence of Charles Wooler as partner for the ageing Sperry. But by the end of the next summer he was on his way home to Rhodesia, Sperry was fading fast, and the county looked to the youngsters Jeff Goodwin and Terry Spencer to form a new opening attack.

Meanwhile, the skipper always had the chance of a few leg-breaks from Gerry Lester. "I don't think Charles thought much of his bowling," Vic Munden maintains. "He really spun it, but he couldn't always drop it. He used to say, 'As soon as I'm hit for four, I'm off. I know that.'"

The first year of Charles' captaincy saw Leicestershire move up just one place in the table, though their three victories, fewer than the bottom side Essex, were the same as in 1949. Charles himself headed the batting averages in all matches while, having arrived at Leicester with just 56 first-class wickets to his name, his medium-paced seamers now brought him 40 more. "We were still a Cinderella side," he reflects. Most importantly, however, his captaincy created a new spirit in the club. "At that stage I was trying to make them feel more confident of themselves. They were all good players, but they hadn't been a team."

Despite the modest results Les Berry could already sense that the corner had been turned. He wrote in the 1951 handbook:

> I believe that Leicestershire cricket has a good chance – perhaps the best in the club's history – of winning a place "on the map" in the next few seasons. The skipper and secretary, Charles Palmer, has thrown himself into the work of reconstruction with tremendous energy and enthusiasm, and under his leadership the county's prospects are brighter than for many years.

The season's most dramatic match came at Westcliff where Essex set the visitors 236 to win and the young Ken Smith, held back to number eleven, came in to face one ball with the score on 230 for nine. It 'sped harmlessly past the off stump' to leave the match drawn, though *Wisden* reckoned that 'the bare result gives no hint of the excitement' in the final stages. The closeness of the contest owed much to a century by the veteran George Watson, though Jeff Goodwin, in one of his first matches, recalls the innings with some ambivalence. "George lost us the match by hitting the ball over the sight screen. It was a park ground, and it landed in a field where the grass was three feet high. Charles was doing his nut because they took ages to find the ball."

At the end of the summer Leicestershire played Surrey at The Oval, with the home side needing victory to share the Championship with Lancashire, their first Championship since 1914. At one stage it looked as if the weather would stand in their way, but the Leicestershire batting collapsed and, with an hour remaining, Surrey were left to score just two runs in their second innings. A large crowd was in the ground, and the Surrey captain Michael Barton recalls how his opposite number decided to introduce a little fun. "Charles said to me, 'You go in first, and I'll bowl to you.' He took a run all the way from the pavilion and bowled a slow full pitch to leg." M.R. Barton, not out, 4. C.H.Palmer, 0.1 – 0 – 4 – 0. Surrey were joint champions.

There were 13 Championship losses for the county in that first season, but none matched the scale of that inflicted by the touring West Indians at Grace Road. Vic Munden, as twelfth man, claims that he was the busiest of the home team's players – because he had to sit alongside the legendary scorer Bill Ferguson and keep the Leicestershire book. He recorded the first wicket at 95 when Jackson, soon after coming on, bowled Allan Rae for 26, but this was not the beginning of a great spell from the Australian. "Vic Jackson had a good cricket brain," Charles chuckles. "A few overs later he strained his back and left the field for the day."

"Jack Walsh wasn't too pleased about that," Vic Munden says, "because he had to take the brunt of the bowling." Roy Marshall, Rae's fellow opener, was already in full flow and now, joining him in the middle, was Frank Worrell who, Vic Munden says, "was like a black panther, a tall lad. He'd been on the rum the previous night and he went in to bat with eyes like a spaniel.

Apparently he said to the fielders as he walked by, 'I'll just play a few shots and get out.'

"He went crash, crash, crash and by the end there was no stopping him. Roy Marshall got 188, but I'd never seen anything like Frank Worrell. And Fergie said, 'That's not the boy to watch, you want to watch the next one in, Everton Weekes.' When he came in, Worrell gave him most of the bowling. Weekes got a hundred in 62 minutes, something like that. Fantastic to watch and in the end Jim Sperry – he was getting towards the end of his career – he was that tired, they were pushing it back nearly to him and running."

Charles carries a different, more laconic, memory of the physical exertion: "At the end of the first day they were 651 for 2, and we never got tired because we never ran after the ball. We only waited for the crowd to throw it back."

He remembers the desperate tactics he used to contain Weekes. "I said to Jim Sperry, 'Jim, bowling a line and length is getting us nowhere; try seven on the offside and bowl well outside the off stump. At this stage he was not averse to advice and was happy to hand over all responsibility. 'OK, skipper,' he replied, 'I'll give it a go.' The ploy certainly had one effect: it reduced the arc for scoring from 360 degrees to 180; it did not, however, reduce the scoring overall as Weekes then ran across to the off side, sometimes as much as four feet, and crashed the ball to the mid-wicket boundary. The umpires were not given the opportunity to award wides! My next idea, that Sperry should adopt the same idea but on the leg side, merely resulted in Weekes running to leg and smashing the ball through the vacant covers."

Charles remembers that they all returned next day, confidently expecting a declaration. "I went into the West Indies dressing room to say good morning to John Goddard and his team. 'We bat on,' he said. I must have failed to hide the horror of my thoughts that it was all going to start again. 'Don't worry,' he said, 'it won't be for long, just until Everton gets his fifth double century of the tour.'" Weekes achieved his goal at 682 for two, while Worrell was unbeaten on 241. Meanwhile, in the pavilion Clyde Walcott sat waiting in vain for a turn to bat.

A century for Les Berry ensured a respectable first innings reply, but after the inevitable follow-on Sonny Ramadhin, with six for 27, made light work of the county's batsmen and the match was lost by an innings and 249 runs.

Amid the early trials of trying to lift an unsuccessful county side Charles found time to remember his young charges at Bromsgrove School. Nigel Sisson, captain of the school team that year, still has the scrapbook in which he pasted a treasured telegram. Dated 12th May 1950 it reads: 'Best wishes to you and yours for the coming season. Charles Palmer.'

Was Charles ever looking wistfully back to life at Bromsgrove? By the end of that first season, did he harbour any regrets at his decision to devote his life and livelihood to cricket? "Oh no, there's always an excitement about a first season, whether it's a bad one or a good one, I think. And we had moved up one place in the table."

TEST CAPTAIN: LEN HUTTON OR BILL EDRICH

By CHARLES BRAY

WHO is to succeed Freddie Brown as England's captain? That is problem No. 1 for the selectors when they meet, as they must do shortly, to choose the team for the first Test at Leeds on June 5.

Maybe Yardley and Co. will dodge the major issue for the time being. The popular Brown is quite prepared to lead England at Leeds and Lords, if required, but has given the selectors the opportunity to build a team for the all-important Australian series next year.

That opportunity should be taken. With all due respect to the Indians we have the chance to "blood" a new captain—the only chance, for there is no overseas tour this winter.

In my opinion two men stand out as far as here to Melbourne for the job providing their current form warrants their selection as players.

Some candidates

They are Len Hutton, a professional, and Bill Edrich a professional turned amateur. Who are the other candidates? Here are some:

Reg Simpson (Notts), a fine player;

Charlie Palmer (Leicestershire), an all-rounder of great ability and a captain of some experience;

Doug Insole (Essex);

Tom Dollery, captain of the champion county.

Youngsters like David Sheppard, Peter May, Donald Carr and the much-improved Guy Willatt.

None I think can compete with either Len Hutton or Bill Edrich for experience of Test cricket, sound knowledge of the finer points of the game, and sheer playing skill.

Hutton would be my first choice. I cannot forget how Brown repeatedly consulted him in Australia, despite the fact that Denis Compton was the official vice-captain.

Dark horse

There is some antipathy to Len in certain quarters on the ground that his is a defensive, cautious outlook. He does not fit in with the craze for brighter cricket.

Yet I have seen him score faster than most when the need demanded it. He has his moods, it is true, but usually there is a sound reason for them.

Bill Edrich looks to be in form this season, and that would make it difficult for the selectors to pass him over, and yet pick the best captain.

Charlie Palmer is my "dark horse" for the captaincy. He is a studious little man, popular with his team, but a stern disciplinarian for all that.

It might be a good idea to let the captaincy go round a bit this season. When all is said and done sound judgment cannot be formed on any if they are not given an opportunity to show what they can do.

Such was Charles Palmer's impact in his first two summers as captain of Leicestershire that his name was being whispered as a 'dark horse' candidate to captain England in the summer of 1952.

CHAPTER 9

THREE DAYS AT THE TOP

The summer of 1951 saw further progress up the County Championship table, from sixteenth to fifteenth. This time there were four victories for Leicestershire, but it could easily have been more if they had not been handicapped by bad weather and a crop of injuries, most crucially to Jack Walsh, who missed half the matches. Charles again topped the averages with 1,694 runs at over 42, Vic Jackson had an outstanding summer with both bat and ball, and there were reasons for hope in the progress of Vic Munden and in the performances of two new signings from Yorkshire, Gerry Smithson and Jack Firth.

Membership income increased by £350 – thanks in no small measure to the chicken dinners Charles had eaten all the previous winter – and £2,800 was spent on improvements to the Grace Road ground. The consequence was a balance sheet with a deficit, but in a statement to the press Charles made clear that they were thinking beyond the challenge of annual survival:

> We are spending heavily, not to avoid liquidation, but with the policy of developing so that we can hold our own with other counties in all respects. There is a firm intention to give Leicestershire a stronger foundation and the emphasis is on expansion. We have a larger staff, a nursery with a coach and have spent a great deal on improving the ground. Within the Club it is felt that for far too long Leicestershire has just kept its head above water and now is the time to gamble its resources and make it flourish as never before.

After a year without a coach, the club had hired the former Kent batsman Bill Ashdown, who was to become a popular figure at Grace Road through the 1950s. "Fantastic bloke," says Freddie Foulds, one of the new intake that year. "We all got on very well with Bill. He never boasted about his achievements. He played with us in the seconds. He used to take his kit out of his bag, and he always put on his cap before he put on any other clothing."

By the following summer, 1952, Leicestershire were clearly on the rise. Charles was now 33 years old, and as a batsman he reached a new peak, becoming the first Leicestershire player since the war to top 2,000 runs in a season. And his side was the most improved in the country, as the *Playfair Cricket Annual* makes clear:

> With their bowling substantially improved by the return to health and form of Walsh, with their batting more consistent, and, above all, with the whole team imbued by Palmer with a spirit of zest and determination, Leicestershire enjoyed their most prosperous season for many years. They had been bottom in 1949, now they finished sixth. Only once – in 1905, when they finished fifth – have they done better.

Maurice Tompkin scored more than 1,800 runs, and he was supported by Gerry Lester and Gerry Smithson. Jack Firth the wicket-keeper established a new county record with 85 victims in the season. But the great strength of the side lay in the fact that four of the six main bowlers – Walsh, Jackson, Munden and Charles himself – were all good enough batsmen to score 1,000 runs. In addition, with Jeff Goodwin fully fit all season and the newcomer Terry Spencer, they had a new ball attack to replace the 42-year-old Jim Sperry and the Rhodesian Charles Wooler, who had gone home.

Terry Spencer would serve the Leicestershire cause through to the 1970s, becoming the third greatest wicket-taker in the county's history. "Charles gave me my chance to become a professional cricketer," he says. "I had three or four weeks with him in the nets in April '52, and he saw a bit of potential. He was a big help in my career. There's a lot that said he bowled me too much but, when you're young and enthusiastic, you don't bother about that."

Terry speaks for others in pointing to Charles' own contribution. "He was a great cricketer: batting, bowling and fielding. He made the club with his ability as a batsman. He encouraged the young players, and he did so much off the field. It was a bit of a gamble for him coming up from Worcestershire, but he turned everything round, really."

In addition to leading Leicestershire up the table, Charles had the honour that summer of playing for the Gentlemen against the Players at Lord's, being called up at the last minute to replace the injured Bill Edrich. It was only his second appearance in the fixture, following his selection in 1948 when the touring party to South Africa had been under consideration.

Lord's had never been a happy ground for him. He had made only 5 and 0 in that 1948 match, and his nine innings there since the start of 1950 had produced just 37 runs, including the only pair of his career – bowled both times by Alan Moss – against Middlesex in May 1951. In the Gentlemen's first innings he was caught Compton, bowled Laker for another nought and, when he emerged from the Long Room the second time, the Players were well on top. With the pitch dusty and, with 323 runs needed for victory, the score was only 54 and already Sheppard, Simpson and Willatt were out. At 73 May drove a ball into his foot and was caught at extra cover and, according to *The Times*, 'there seemed only one possible ending.'

Doug Insole, the Essex captain, was next to the wicket. With a penchant for working the ball to leg, he was a batsman whose technique was quite different from Charles', and together they added 105 in quick time. It was a partnership that allowed EW Swanton to compare the two of them:

has shown how far nerve, a keen eye and good wrists will take a young man of good physique.

Palmer's method has a neatness and polish that makes him a real pleasure to watch. It can be said of him that he "puts a bloom on the orthodox." He played all the strokes. The best was the force off his legs that sent the ball with a clean and a late turn of the wrists humming past the square leg boundary.

'A real pleasure to watch.' In due course Charles would have his differences with the *Daily Telegraph*'s cricket correspondent, but this report appears in Swanton's anthology 'As I Said At The Time', under the heading 'A Great Innings by C.H. Palmer', and Charles knows the page number by heart.

He and Insole scampered between the wickets, even running six when one of Charles' late cuts pulled up just short of the boundary at the Nursery end with Jim Laker in less than hot pursuit. Eventually the new ball was taken, and Insole departed at 178, then Trevor Bailey at 235.

There were 88 runs wanted in less than an hour, when Bailey was replaced by the former England captain Freddie Brown. For *The Times* it was a case of 'the right man at the right hour. With fierce straight drives, lofted hits and quick runs against an expanded field, he and Palmer – now past his most worthy 100 – set the scoreboard singing a merry tune.'

They reached 305 for six with 18 minutes remaining, but in quick succession they both fell, Charles for 127. There were some further brave hits and, when Laker began the final over, the last Gentlemen pair needed just three runs for victory. In the previous Laker over Robin Marlar 'had smacked him to the boundary', but his attempt to repeat the stroke off the over's first ball saw his wicket demolished. The Players had won by two runs, the closest finish in the fixture since W.G. Grace had carried his bat to a one-wicket victory in 1896.

Early the following week Charles received a letter from Sir Pelham Warner, the Grand Old Man of English cricket, who two years earlier had written a comprehensive history of Gentlemen/Players matches.

Dear Palmer,

Allow me to offer you my warmest congratulations on your great innings at Lord's today. You batted superbly and your lovely off drives and the way in which you picked the ball off your toes will remain in my memory.

Yours was one of the best innings I have seen in a Gentlemen v Players match and I have seen a very large number.

What a match.

With my best wishes and again my congratulations on an innings which those who saw it will not forget.

Yours,

PF Warner

Leicestershire, The Oval, 1953

Standing (from left): Freddie Parker (twelfth man), Jack Firth, Gerry Smithson, Vic Munden, Maurice Tompkin, Don Goodson, Maurice Hallam, Jeff Goodwin, Walter Goodenough (scorer)

Sitting: Vic Jackson, Gerry Lester, Charles Palmer, Jack Walsh

The following summer of 1953 saw the Leicestershire team reassemble in buoyant mood. Terry Spencer's appearances would be restricted by National Service, but the rest of the side – including the promising young batsman Maurice Hallam – would turn out in almost all the matches.

Charles Palmer batting against the 1953 Australians

The summer began with a two-day defeat by the Australians, followed by four championship matches in which they lost two and drew two. Charles was the only batsman to make runs against the Australians and he also recorded the only double century of his career at Northampton, but the highlight of these early matches was undoubtedly the last day at Portsmouth. Hampshire had built a first innings lead of 279 and, when Charles stepped out on the final morning with Terry Spencer, the Leicester second innings stood at 81 for seven. "The previous evening," Charles remembers, "I had been dropped before I scored, by Desmond Eagar at short leg. And I was on a pair."

With Jack Walsh nursing a dislocated finger and unable to bat, there was only Jeff Goodwin to come and he was, by his own admission, "one of the worst number elevens playing cricket." In part, he puts this down to the way Bill Ashdown, the coach, got him to think about his batting. "He used to say, 'Quick bowlers, your job is to get wickets. Go out there, swing the bat and get out.' No matter what state the game is in, nine, ten, jack it's your job to have a swing because you're wanted for your bowling."

There was no expectation of the day's play lasting long, and the team's thoughts turned to the train journey home. "Vic Jackson went off to phone the station to find out what time the earliest train was," Jeff Goodwin remembers. "But Terry Spencer stopped with Charles till lunchtime. Then, when he got out and I went in, there was Vic going off to find out what time the next train was."

'No matter what state the game is in, it's your job to have a swing.' But Charles met Jeff Goodwin and had other advice for him. "He said, 'Make them fight for your wicket!'"

And fight, they did. For two hours and ten minutes they fought and, with interruptions for rain as well, it was enough to save them from defeat. 'In the final 15 minutes of a grand day's cricket,' *The Times* reported, 'Palmer farmed the bowling cleverly and kept Goodwin away from Shackleton and Cannings.' Goodwin's unbeaten 23 was the highest score of his 167-innings career while Charles came off to 'a generous and well deserved ovation' with 102.

Jeff recalls the hapless Hampshire skipper: "Desmond Eagar, I can see him now, jumping up and down, tearing his hair out." And Derek Shackleton, who bowled most of the day on his favourite United Services Ground wicket, is on record as saying that he 'cannot recall any other occasion when a genuine tail-ender lasted so long' against him.

The first victory of the season came in late May at Grace Road, when the 21-year-old Maurice Hallam, already in his 22nd match for the county, finally got beyond a score of 34, top-scoring in each innings with 77 and 46. "I went in at number eight in the first innings," he used to tell, "and I was playing absolutely terribly. I turned to Andy Wilson, the Gloucestershire keeper. 'I'm playing like an idiot,' I said. 'Just look at the scoreboard,' he replied. I had 20-odd against my name. 'Keep your head; you'll be fine.' I made 77. And I never got out of the side from then on."

Ten days later they were pressing for a second victory against a Sussex side revitalised by the dynamic captaincy of David Sheppard. On the final day Leicestershire were batting for a second time, with their lead well past 300, but Charles was reluctant to declare too soon. At Bristol he had set Gloucestershire 302 to win in four hours 20 minutes, and they had won with time to spare. He was determined to set a tougher target this time.

"It's about time they declared," the Sussex captain muttered to his teammates. Away in the scorebox the discs were going up, indicating that a new ball could soon be taken. After 55 overs, there was a white disc. At 60, a yellow one. Then at 65 both appeared and, with the lead now 345 and only four hours of batting time left, David Sheppard turned to Jim Wood, his left-arm opening bowler. "Take the new ball," he said, "but don't take it out of its wrapping. Have a couple of practice run-ups. I'll re-set the field for you."

With exaggerated deliberation the Sussex captain made fine adjustments to his men's positions. Then, in the words of Rupert Webb, the wicket-keeper, "Charlie Palmer appeared. A little man. He didn't walk down the stairs. He came tumbling down, in a great hurry. And he waved the batsmen in."

David Sheppard turned to his Sussex team as they walked off together. "I knew they couldn't afford a new ball," he said.

A target of 346 in just under four hours, no county had successfully chased so many in the past five years. But Sheppard was in determined mood, and he hit an unbeaten and chanceless 186 – "the most exciting innings I ever played," he reckoned – and Sussex won with minutes to spare.

A week later, still seeking their second victory of the summer, they were at Bath, where the newly relaid square had already led to one match ending in a day. Somerset had a new off-spinner, 17-year-old Brian Langford, and his 11 wickets in the match brought his tally to 25 in a week. But Vic Munden proved his equal, his second innings 53 the top score on either side and his match figures of ten wickets for 42 bringing a welcome victory.

"When we finished, I was expecting a bit of praise," he now admits. "These days people gets hugs and kisses every time they get a wicket. But all Charles said was, 'You have done well, my friend.' That's all he said."

In a wet summer Leicestershire reached the halfway point of their championship programme with only three victories, but a further seven would follow in the second half.

They won at Worcester in Roly Jenkins' benefit match, though Roly himself was unable to play. "Roly was a bit round the twist," Jeff Goodwin says, "but a brilliant bowler. There was one match when I was batting and suddenly he took off his boots and put them behind the stumps. Their captain said, 'What are you doing, Roly?' Roly said, 'I'm going to try bowling without these boots.' It was the same with Bomber Wells. He used to take one boot off. Don't ask me why."

They won at Grace Road in the Bank Holiday derby against Northants, when Charles and Maurice Tompkin, needing 311, came together at 99 for two. Freddie Brown was the Northants captain, and he tested the pair of them with the pace of a young Frank Tyson and the teasing guile of the Australian slow left-armer George Tribe. But Tompkin finished with 143, Charles with 96, and they returned together to the pavilion victorious.

Then in the next match they won a thrilling victory against Yorkshire, with Vic Munden bowling at the death to a belligerent Fred Trueman. Nine wickets were down and in Munden's previous over Trueman had struck three successive boundaries, but Charles retained faith in his slow left-arm bowler. When Trueman hit a fourth four, the bowler began to fear the worst. "I thought, 'Oh dear, they only want six more to win and that's it.' The next ball he tried to hit me again, but he missed it and Firthy stumped him. So we'd won by six runs. Fred said it wasn't out. We were walking off and the crowd were cheering us all because we'd just beaten the Yorkies, and Fred bustled his way through and he said, "If that effer was out, my prick's a kipper!"

Not since 1934 had a home crowd in Leicestershire been able to cheer a victory over Yorkshire, and now the county was in third place in the table. Then at Loughborough they beat Kent and held on for a draw against fellow title contenders Surrey. On Friday 21st August, they were back at Grace Road, and victory over Essex would take them to the top of the table.

They wanted 243 to win, and at 142 for five they looked unlikely to get there. But, reported *The Times*, 'the turning point was a sixth wicket stand of 65 between Munden and Jackson'. Then, against 'a background of thunder and lightning', wickets fell and Jackson found himself partnered by Terry Spencer, eight wickets down and still another 13 runs wanted.

Jeff Goodwin was the only batsman to come, and he remembers waiting nervously. "I know Maurice Tompkin was down in the toilets," he says.

'Spencer's defence against every delivery was cheered enthusiastically and Jackson, coolly exploiting his favourite cut, steered the score to 239.' Only four runs were now needed as Ray Smith bowled to Spencer, and the tall tail-ender 'glanced him to the boundary for the winning stroke.'

According to *The Times*, 'exultant spectators mobbed the pair' though 'the players had not reached the dressing room before a heavy storm saturated the wicket.' For the first time in the history of the club, Leicestershire stood on top of the championship table.

CHAMPIONSHIP TABLE – 21 AUGUST 1953

		Played	Won	Drawn	Tied	Lost	Points
1	Leicestershire	26	10	10	0	6	152
2	Middlesex	26	10	11	1	4	150
3	Surrey	24	10	10	0	4	148

Celebrations in the dressing room when Leicestershire hit the top

They stayed there for only three days, losing by ten wickets at Trent Bridge. In the final match they managed a draw against Glamorgan, and this left them in third place, the highest championship position in their history.

ILLUSTRATED
LEICESTER CHRONICLE

ESTABLISHED 1810

REGISTERED AS
A NEWSPAPER

SATURDAY, AUGUST 22, 1953

TWOPENCE

No. 1499   New Series

Team Of 100 per cent Triers

SECRET OF SUCCESS

Club as secretary and captain in 1950, the County were used to being a footnut at the bottom of the table. Palmer may not look the part—at twenty-three, but his tenacity was filled to overflow, and made of a team that was in danger of becoming a laughing stock, a force to be reckoned with—now third in the championship, and fighting for the lead.

He has not done this alone. There has been imaginative support and good committee work to back him up, but he has been the playing inspiration on the field. He has brought the crowd clicking through the turnstiles, he has encouraged his team up the table, HE HAS GIVEN BACK TO THE COUNTY SIDE ITS SELF RESPECT.

The county cricket team is of importance to the prestige of the city and county.

Yorkshire can no longer scorn Leicestershire. Palmer leads a team of giant killers. Last year they were sixth. This season they have proved this not to be a flash in the pan.

As a tribute to this fine play, the ILLUSTRATED LEICESTER CHRONICLE asked Charles Palmer to write of the team's success and prospects. Characteristically he plays down his own part in the resurrection.

By Charles Palmer

I THINK it is of paramount importance that we are a happy side—there is not a single black sheep. Every member of the side tries 100 per cent to give his best, and so my job as captain is simplified by needing only to think of how to use our resources to the best advantage on the field.

This happy state of affairs has practical and tactical advantages because it means I can readily ask advice of any of the players. More than that, it means that players can offer me advice on points if they consider I have missed anything. This leads to everyone being always "in the game" and always trying.

THE LEICESTERSHIRE SIDE MAY ALMOST CLAIM TO BE A SIDE OF ALL-ROUNDERS—JACKSON, WALSH, MUNDEN AND MYSELF WITH LESTER IF NECESSARY

Jack Firth, apart from being in my opinion the number two wicket keeper in the country, is no mean performer with the bat. This set-up gives a great flexibility to the side. If the batsmen purely and simply fail (as we all do at times), then several of the bowlers can stage a recovery.

Wealth Of Young Players

If the bowlers fail, then the men who are primarily batsmen can come on and take the wickets. I do not think there has been an out and out failure among the regular players this year. Moreover, the types of bowlers and batsmen we have are of sufficient variety to help us to adapt our methods according to the changeable conditions of English cricket.

It is encouraging to note that the experienced core of the side is really in its prime with many years of cricket still to come, and there is sufficient youth in the side for a reasonable optimism that the present good cycle will continue for several years.

Hallam, Munden, Smithson, Goodwin, Spencer and Boshier are all bound to improve with experience, and there is considerable promising material on the nursery staff under the able tuition of Bill Ashdown, to whom much credit must go.

(Continued on back page.)

Top, circle: Cricket is essentially a game for quiet appreciation. Note these cricket followers at this week's game against Essex, whose expression of patience is equalled only by that of the dog Above: The game is not exclusive to the elder brethren

It was another summer of success for Charles: 1,645 runs, 31 economical wickets and a leadership that had taken the county in successive years from 17th to 16th to 15th to 6th and now to 3rd place in the table. 'A leader without flourish,' the *Playfair Annual* called him, 'but indeed a leader.'

It was therefore no surprise that his name was being considered at Lord's for higher duties. Needing to appoint a manager for their winter tour, the original recommendation of the MCC's West Indies Tour Sub-Committee had been for Billy Griffith, then Assistant Secretary at Lord's and a man with previous experience of the Caribbean. However, the Secretary had felt strongly that 'he could not carry on the administration of the Club's affairs satisfactorily if he was deprived of Mr SC Griffith's services for four months of the year.' There was an attempt to enlist John Nash, Secretary of Yorkshire, before, on 17th August, just as Leicestershire were approaching the top of the championship table, it was recommended that 'Mr CH Palmer, Captain and Secretary of Leicestershire, be invited to accompany the team as manager.'

Although MCC's minutes make no reference to Charles' participation as a player, the decision to take him as a player-manager was prompted by the refusal of the West Indies Board to meet the cost of a sixteenth player. The twin assignment was not a role for which either Griffith, now retired as a wicket-keeper, or Nash would have been fitted.

"I think it was Freddie Brown who had a word with me first," says Charles. Was there a chance he could be spared to go? And if so, could he go as player-manager? Brown, with whom he had had such an exhilarating partnership the previous summer in the Gentlemen/Players match, was now Chairman of Selectors and, though Charles can remember few details of the conversation, he does recall that he needed no time to consider his response. Leicestershire were pleased and proud to find ways of covering his absence; and once he knew that there was a playing role for him, he saw a tour of West Indies as another, probably final, chance to play Test cricket.

Moreover, he says that whether he had been asked to go as a player, as manager or as player-manager, his answer would have been the same. He had had a taste of touring when he had gone to South Africa with George Mann's team. It had been a wonderful six months in the sun. Here was a chance to do it all again and to see a new, unexplored part of the world. He could not wait!

Hindsight would question the wisdom of asking anyone to combine the increasingly onerous role of manager with that of player. In less challenging times, when MCC had last toured the Caribbean, Billy Griffith had fulfilled both roles; so reactions to the appointment foresaw few problems in store for Charles when he bade farewell to his Leicestershire office, leaving behind the man who would serve as his assistant and then succeed him, Tony Diment.

The pair would later become great friends, but they had barely met when Charles set off for the Caribbean. "I literally walked into the office," Tony now recalls, "and Charles said, 'I'm going. Enjoy yourself.'"

CHAPTER 10

A TOUR TO FORGET

If Charles set off for the Caribbean expecting an easy-going tour such as the one to South Africa five years earlier, he was soon to be disabused. Even the journey out was fraught.

"We flew out on a BOAC Stratocruiser, the first time an MCC tour party had ever flown, and that was quite a to-do. We had to fly to Gander in Newfoundland and, in order to have enough fuel, we had to put down in Ireland to replace what we'd used from London."

They were scheduled to spend a night in a hotel in Gander but, Tom Graveney recalls, this did not work out. "In the middle of the night they woke us up and said, 'If you don't get out now, you won't get out for a fortnight.' A big blizzard was on its way. So at one or two o'clock in the morning, we packed all our bags and got back on the plane."

They arrived in Bermuda a few days before Christmas, where the schedule was for them to play three warm-up matches before moving on to Jamaica. It was intended to be a relaxing introduction to the tour, but for Charles the problems of the Caribbean were taxing him as soon as he stepped off the plane. "We found that there was a colour bar in Bermuda, which I hadn't been told about. I met my counterpart at the airport, a Bermudian, and the first thing I wanted to talk about with him was the conditions of play and all that sort of thing. We were standing there with thousands of people milling around, and I said, 'Well let's not talk about it here. Come back to the hotel, and we can talk about it in an armchair.' And people then started semaphoring: 'Not allowed to fraternise. ... Black and white. ... Not at the hotel.' We had to arrange a special meeting elsewhere."

Such a colour bar did not exist in other parts of the West Indies, but the racial sensitivities were every bit as acute. Since Indian Independence six years earlier, home rule movements had grown rapidly throughout the British Commonwealth and, as soon as they arrived, the English tourists were made aware of the feelings of the white people in the islands. For Charles and for other surviving members of the party, it is their dominant memory of this unhappy tour.

"All these countries were saying, 'We want our independence'. And the white people, who had ruled the roost over there for many years, saw the ground crumbling under their feet. Every day on the tour we were being invited to social functions, invariably with the white people, and it was difficult to refuse. And all the time they would be saying to us, 'For God's sake, beat these people, or our lives won't be worth living.' It became a big millstone round our necks. We were almost afraid to talk to a white person. We knew what they were going to say. We wanted to win, but not for them. After a while it ate into our souls."

The arrival of the MCC party

"I'd been brought up to believe that colour was immaterial," Trevor Bailey says, "but I soon discovered that this outlook was far too naïve for the West Indies, where degrees of colour were considered so vital."

Selection of the West Indian Test team was bedevilled by inter-island rivalries, with the captaincy, given briefly to George Headley on the previous tour, now regarded as the preserve of a white man. The captain for this series was Jeffrey Stollmeyer, the son of a cocoa-planter whose grandfather - an anti-slavery campaigner - had migrated to Trinidad from Philadelphia. In the subtle mix of the Caribbean races he was, in Charles' words, "certainly more white than black".

"It was the fag end of white supremacy," says Alex Bannister, who was reporting the tour for the *Daily Mail*. "'If ever we have a black captain,' the white people would say, 'that will be the end of Test cricket in the West Indies.'"

"It was important to the blacks to win as well," Charles adds. "Cricket was their religion. But it wasn't a matter of life and death for them, as it was with the whites. And we didn't fraternise much with them, other than the team and their immediate associates."

West Indies had won when the two teams had last met in England three years earlier so, with England having just beaten Australia to win back the Ashes, the local newspapers were quick to bill the series as for the Cricket Championship of the World. This further raised the temperature.

For previous tours of the Caribbean MCC had sent out half-strength sides, but this time the only concession was to give Alec Bedser a winter's rest with an arduous Ashes tour in prospect. And, for the first time on a full MCC tour, the side was to be captained by a professional, Len Hutton.

"Some of the white people were terrible snobs," Alex Bannister says. "The first day I was at the bar with one or two of the other boys. One of the locals came up and asked each of us which school we'd been to. He came up to me and said, 'Where did you go to school?' I said 'Watford Grammar School.' So he said, 'I can tell by your accent that you're a grammar school boy.' That was the clouded, insular mind that they had.

"And of course they were all against a professional captain. They thought it was a humiliation for them to be the first to have a professional captain sent out from England."

Charles Palmer (far right) sits through a speech in Bermuda

Six years earlier, when MCC had last visited the West Indies, the 45-year-old Gubby Allen, a former England captain in Australia and already a long-established member of the MCC committee, had been appointed both to captain and to manage the tour, with one of his players, the Sussex secretary Billy Griffith, to assist him with the duties of management.

By contrast, this time there was no assistant manager, and Charles was required to combine the roles of managing the tour and taking orders on playing matters from the captain. "It was a two-fisted thing. Sometimes, as a player, I was subordinate to the captain, and sometimes he was subordinate to me. I didn't think it was a good thing at all. I certainly wrote in my report at the end of the tour that it should never happen again."

A slight, bespectacled figure, a player younger than his captain, Charles hardly looked a figure of authority. Nor did he have the Oxbridge or public school background to which the expatriate society attached such disproportionate importance. Was this perhaps why, as MCC manager, he was totally ignored by officials in Jamaica and never spoken to throughout the tour by the Chairman of the West Indies Board? "It could have been a contribution to the problem," Alex Bannister feels.

It seems that Hutton himself, perhaps realising how heavy a responsibility was being placed on him as a professional cricketer, had wanted Billy Griffith to be his manager, but Griffith was now MCC's Assistant Secretary and could not be spared. So Charles had been chosen, and he was soon finding that the introverted Yorkshireman took some understanding.

"At first with Len I didn't know whether I was coming or going, because he always answered a question by posing another one. And I thought, 'How the hell am I going to live with this for three months, with him fending all these questions off?' But the more I knew him and the more we had to go through adversity together, the more I got to like him. In fact, I got to respect him and to like him, two very different things."

For MCC, all tours carried the responsibility of spreading goodwill from the mother country to the nations of the Commonwealth. "The in-built ethos," Charles recalls, "was, 'You're going out to represent your country, and you've got to behave yourselves.'" But for Len Hutton, a professional cricketer, there was also an in-built assumption that he was being asked to win the series. "Len asked for fewer social occasions," Alex Bannister says. "He'd been there in 1948 and he said the most tiring thing about it was having, after a day's cricket, to go to a social gathering. It was always the same people there, half of whom had got nothing to speak about and knew nothing about cricket; and the other half were the people who did know about cricket and they would be pressing their opinions. You can understand why it was so wearisome."

"It was always the white people at the social functions," Charles says, "and there was never a day when there wasn't a function to go to. It was very difficult to refuse them, particularly as they were looking to us to help them. Len was quite right in saying, 'Let's have less of them.'"

Unfortunately, as early as the Jamaican leg of the tour, this reluctance to be sociable at the end of the day started to cause offence, not only to the white people who were laying on the functions but also to the West Indian cricketers themselves who were keen to renew the friendships they had made in England in 1950. Hutton's instinct was to approach the series much as a Yorkshireman would approach a Roses match.

Hutton always maintained that he placed no embargo on mixing with the opposition, but that is not the impression he gave to all his team-mates. According to Godfrey Evans, 'He said to us, in effect: "Well, we've got to do these people, haven't we? We've got to do 'em. You mustn't speak to 'em on or off the field. Keep right away from 'em, don't take any notice of what they say. Get stuck right into the job and beat 'em at all costs."'

When Frank Worrell met up for the first time with the England players, he was shocked by the monosyllabic responses that returned his greetings. 'I was beginning to wonder whether I had been the victim of one of Clyde Walcott's practical jokes,' he wrote, 'but I soon learned I hadn't. Clyde and Everton Weekes told me that they had been trying, ever since the MCC party arrived a week previously, to do everything in their power to entertain our guests, but they had received the same treatment.'

Further difficulties arose when, by popular subscription, the 44-year-old George Headley, the great Jamaican batsman of the 1930s, was brought back from England. "It was a mistake, really," Charles says, "but it's what the people of Jamaica wanted." In his first innings, playing for Combined Parishes against the tourists, Headley was struck a painful blow on the elbow by a Fred Trueman bouncer and was forced to retire. The young fast bowler thereby earned his first black mark of the tour; the second quickly followed when he walked back to his mark, showing no concern for the local hero.

There were further repercussions to this in the first Test when Headley came out to bat just before lunch on the second day. As if it were the great man's benefit match Hutton set the field back, allowing Headley to push an easy single off his first ball from Brian Statham. According to EW Swanton, reporting for *The Daily Telegraph*, it was 'a most agreeable gesture', but the result of it was that Headley then had to face the last over before lunch from Trueman, an over that contained several bumpers.

In the view of Clyde Walcott, who was batting at the other end, the episode 'probably caused more resentment than any other single incident on the tour.' Hutton sought to clarify matters by saying that he had given the single for old time's sake, because it was obviously going to be George Headley's last Test, and, given the atmosphere that had already developed on the tour, every possible interpretation of the sequence of events seemed to cause offence. Either he was lying and determined to subject Headley to Trueman's bumpers, or he was unnecessarily patronising the great West Indian.

Trueman was often at the centre of such storms, both on the field and off. "Dear old Fred," Charles says now. "I have grown to like him. But he was on his first tour and he spoke as a Yorkshireman would speak in Yorkshire. It was not really his fault. He was catapulted into a society of which he had no experience whatsoever; and he was unable to adapt to different customs, different accents and whatever. I remember in a bar one night. This fellow came up. He said he had a friend in Yorkshire and did Fred know him? And instead of Fred saying, 'No, but I'll look out for him' or some such words, he said, 'Never 'eard of the bugger.' They were little things, but they didn't go down very well in a highly sensitive situation."

"He was a bit of a nuisance because he never stopped talking," Alex Bannister says, "but there was nothing malicious in him. He was a young Yorkshireman on his first tour, and I don't think he'd been given any instructions from his family or anyone else that might have stopped him talking. They probably didn't understand his humour out there."

The first Test was a disaster for England in every respect. Hutton had issued instructions to his batsmen to cut out all risky strokes and, despite the presence of Compton, May and Graveney in the side, their first innings total of 170 took almost 90 overs. In the second, when Watson made a valiant 116, their rate of scoring was not much faster and they lost by 140 runs.

There were problems, too, for the umpires. On the second day Jamaica's JK Holt, playing his first Test in front of his home crowd, had reached 94 when he was hit on the back leg by a low, straight ball from Statham and was given lbw by umpire Perry Burke. Later Burke was accosted by a man with a knife while his father, wife and son were all subjected to threats or actual physical attack. As the tour progressed, the tourists themselves became victims of several controversial decisions, and a feeling developed among the party that the local umpires were being influenced by the partisan crowds.

"If you've got an umpire who's going to need bodily protection to get off the ground at the end of the day," Charles says, "and also when he's at home, and there are threats against his wife and children, then they won't want to put a foot wrong. I would never accuse them of cheating. Indeed I made a point of this in my report to the MCC. They were just incompetent. They hadn't the experience."

The report itself confirms this:

> The umpiring has been the subject of much controversy. I wish to deny any allegations that we have assumed dishonesty. We have said that the standard of umpiring at times has not been good. We do not expect umpires who umpire infrequently to match the general standard attained by English umpires who do the job six days a week professionally and who are most likely old first-class cricketers of considerable experience. Furthermore, we realize that the umpiring out here is much more difficult than in England because an umpire here has long periods in the sun which tends to weaken his concentration, and because in places he often works before partisan, noisy and at times even menacing crowds. By analysis we consider that mistakes have been made more against than for MCC (and I repeat this does not imply dishonesty).

Yet another element was added to the mix in the West Indian second innings when Tony Lock sent down his quicker ball and umpire Burke called him for throwing. Not long previously, he had ended George Headley's Test career with a similar delivery. "Poor George," Alex Bannister says. "He was well over forty, and he didn't even see it."

In the next first-class match, against Barbados, Lock was called twice in three deliveries, and after that he did not bowl his faster ball. In the Jamaican Test he had taken five wickets for 112 runs; in the remaining four Tests, he took only nine for 606 runs. 'The no-balling caused quite a rumpus,' Jim Laker wrote. 'Yet to my eyes his quickest ball was a genuine throw, and it looked glaring in Barbados.'

As in South Africa, Charles had brought a cine camera with him, though this time his duties as the manager of a demanding tour made it difficult for him to find much time for photography. But he does have footage of the Barbados match, and a sequence of frames confirms Laker's judgement. "It certainly shows up Tony Lock's action," Charles says more diplomatically. Alas, there is no film of Hutton's innings in the match, an innings of 59 not out which has stayed in Charles' memory for fifty years. Hutton was not well and had put himself down to bat at number eight. Then, when he went out to bat with MCC struggling, he found that John Goddard was bowling off-spin and had set a field to prevent his off-side shots. "And he gave this wonderful exhibition of cricketing nous. Normally he would always play in the same way, with a sort of divine inevitability. But on this occasion he cow-shotted it, hit the ball with a cross bat. He took risks, all calculated. It was a marvellous innings."

England had played the first Test with four pace bowlers, Statham, Trueman, Bailey and Alan Moss, with Lock providing the only spin. But the heavy defeat led to a rethink for the second Test. A more balanced attack and a shorter tail were the two recipes for improvement.

Trueman and Moss were both omitted, with Laker picked as a second spinner. The front-line attack therefore comprised Statham, Bailey, Lock and Laker, and this left a place for an extra batsman. 'It might be possible,' EW Swanton wrote, 'to give one of the doubtful places on grounds of general utility to Palmer.'

Up to this point Charles had batted only once in a first-class match, scoring 33 against Jamaica before being harshly given out lbw. If the selectors, of whom he was one along with Hutton, Bailey and Compton, had entertained thoughts similar to Swanton's, it was paramount that the player-manager should play in the match against Barbados, which preceded the Test. But he was not chosen.

Instead, Ken Suttle, the uncapped youngster taken on the tour in preference to Bill Edrich and Reg Simpson, was given another game and, opening the batting, he top-scored with 96 and 62. Although Swanton thought that he made his runs 'without ever looking happy with his timing', Suttle had laid a powerful claim for a place in the Test team.

However, Hutton was not an admirer of the young batsman, knowing that his inclusion in the tour party had owed too much to a single century at Lord's in front of Sir Pelham Warner. He felt that the party had been chosen in too much haste, and he remained unconvinced that Suttle would make runs at the highest level.

So it was that, when the four selectors met, Charles was asked to leave the room. "When I came back in, they told me that I was included in the side. And I hadn't had a bat in my hand for three weeks." So should they not have made sure that he had been given a chance for practice in the colony match? "Absolutely," says Charles. "I would concur with that. But suddenly there was this decision to play me, so I had a quick net and then went into the match." In the event Charles was not called upon to bowl in West Indies' first innings, when the home team made 383, thanks largely to a hard-hit 220 from Clyde Walcott. "He'd got tree trunks, not arms. You dared not stand in the way of the ball. He really did hit it hard. In fact, he murdered the ball. The only batsman I can remember hitting the ball harder than Walcott was Wally Hammond, in one of my first matches before the war. I fielded at cover point to him and, oh boy, you really didn't want to field the ball. Everton Weekes gave it a bit of a tonk square, but Clyde Walcott hit it straight. And Frank Worrell, he stroked it. He'd got grace. He was a charming man, and it showed itself in his cricket."

The first day, a Saturday, closed with the West Indies on 258 for five, but any thought Charles had of a quiet rest day quickly evaporated when he found himself dealing with another incident at the hotel. At the end of a boisterous Saturday evening there had been some high spirits in the lift, including some colourful language, and it fell to Charles to sort out a complaint from two ladies, also in the lift, one of whom Swanton described as 'holding forth in a fine, manly baritone, rather in the manner of Bertie Wooster's Aunt Agatha'. Though they have always claimed that it was a case of mistaken identity, Trueman - whose birthday it had been - and Lock were the suspects.

Walcott continued to his double century on Monday morning. The pitch was described by *Wisden* as 'ideal for batting' but, in the thirty overs till close of play, Hutton's strategy of crease occupation left England on only 53 for two. The following day they progressed to 181 for nine, adding 128 runs in 114 overs, most of them sent down by the spinners Ramadhin and Valentine.

"Ram and Val didn't turn it so much out there," Charles says. "Over here they'd turned it square. Some of the pitches out there were bone hard, like marble. You'd have a job to turn a ball before three days. On those sorts of wickets they were better bowlers than we were."

The elegant Tom Graveney spent two hours in the middle. "Ram was bowling when I came in," he recalls, "and I hit the first two like a rocket: one at mid-off, one at mid-on. A yard either side, and I would have had eight runs. And Len walked down the wicket. 'We don't want any of that,' he said. I got 15 in two hours and miscued a full toss straight back to the bowler."

With the score on 107 for four, Charles was stepping out to play his first Test innings. Surrounded by close fielders, he was rapped on the pads by Ramadhin's first ball but survived. Next ball he was off the mark. "I can remember batting at the far end from the pavilion," he says, "and to my astonishment I hit a four." It was a cover drive and, in Swanton's view, it was 'just about the best stroke of the innings.'

"Len Hutton treated Ramadhin as an off-spinner," Charles explains. "If it went the other way, he was safe. But sometimes, when it pitched middle-and-leg, it put you in an awkward position. He was a mystery man. I found him extremely difficult." And how did he compare with the more recent Muralitharan? "Oh, I wouldn't know what to do with that bloke," Charles says. "I think I'd give up the game."

At the other end Hutton had progressed to 64 but, perhaps taunted by a restless crowd chanting 'We want our money back' and 'We want cricket', his patience suddenly snapped and he twice lofted Valentine for four. Then he tried a third time, but the ball held up in the wind for Ramadhin to take a fine catch.

Charles was joined by Trevor Bailey and, according to Swanton, their partnership of 39 was 'the only stand of the innings that reflected much credit on the batting side.' Then Charles, with his score on 22, snicked a Ramadhin leg-break to slip. "I was caught out brilliantly by Walcott." According to Swanton, 'it was one of the few occasions in the day when the bat was properly and genuinely beaten by a good ball.'

The West Indies took a first innings lead of 202 and, thanks to a score of 166 by Holt, they were able to declare on 292 for two in their second innings. Amid the West Indian run feast Charles was finally given a bowl, and Swanton records that he should have taken a wicket: 'He suddenly varied his medium-pace with a slow leg-spinner which Worrell chased and missed well down the wicket. Evans, astonishingly, missed the ball altogether and it went for three byes.' "I didn't spin it," Charles says with typical self-deprecation. "How it happened, I don't know, but it was a beautiful leg-spinner."

England needed 495 to win and, according to Denis Compton, this was the point when some of the senior players talked Hutton out of his batting strategy. 'In the First Test,' he wrote, 'we seemed to play our cricket in handcuffs, and the first innings at Barbados was even worse. It was paralysed cricket. It was time, I pointed out, to throw away our chains and to allow the stroke players to play the game their own way. Len said that he wouldn't interfere with such a policy, and so a new plan went into operation. We were to attack, and attack we did.'

At close of play they had 214 for three, with Hutton, May and Compton all making runs, and there seemed just a chance of an unlikely victory. But next morning Compton was judged lbw on 93, and immediately Charles was out for a duck, to another good catch, as he attempted to drive to leg. Though Tom Graveney batted well, the match was lost by 181 runs, and England were 2-0 down in the series.

"We played like absolute twits in the first two Test matches," Charles says. "We were terrible, and we deservedly lost both of them. But, of course, it put the whites right on the back foot, so they didn't like us at all."

In British Guiana England would revert to playing an extra bowler, picking Johnny Wardle, so that Charles' one-match Test career was over. "I can't really remember anything very significant about it," he now says. "I went in with the conscious or unconscious idea that I was only a stooge, filling in because they wanted to make a change. I hadn't any thought that I had got in on merit. Because I had done nothing to get in on merit. I can confirm that it was a tenser atmosphere than one found in an ordinary county match. The ceiling seemed to be a little bit nearer to one's head. I didn't notice anything in the fielding or even in the bowling. It was just in the batting that it seemed to be slightly different."

Before they had even set off for British Guiana, Charles found that another rumpus had developed, this one involving Tom Graveney and a cocktail party, which included some officers from a couple of Royal Navy destroyers in the harbour.

"We were feeling pretty sorry for ourselves, having lost the first two Tests," Tom Graveney says. "And we gave it the run that night. We enjoyed ourselves; we had a bit of a party. Then late in the evening one bloke came up to me and said, 'Your team won't be any good until you stop Evans, Compton and Bailey drinking.' To which I gave a suitable reply, let's put it like that!"

The next morning at breakfast he was greeted by Penny Robins, daughter of Test selector Walter Robins and on the tour as Charles' secretary. "She said, 'What were you doing last night?' I said, 'Nothing. I had a good night.' 'Well, Charles and Len are up at Government House, trying to save you from being sent home.' I said, 'What on earth for?' 'Apparently you had a go at one of the guests at the cocktail party.' Then I found that the bloke I'd crossed swords with was staying at Government House, a friend of the Governor."

"The Governor-Generals were like gods in their own worlds," Charles says, recalling that the actual complaint came from a lady at the party. "Somehow she was persuaded that she was talking a load of codswallop. There was absolutely no question of Tom being sent home. Tom was a super tourist."

Life grew no easier in British Guiana. The state match saw free-flowing double centuries from both Willie Watson and Tom Graveney. "Watson was lovely to watch," Charles says. "He never moved, he glided. He never ran, he was never in a hurry. He was a smooth performer in every way."

But the tourists were again unhappy with the standard of umpiring, requesting two different officials for the Test match. However, hopes that more experienced umpires might be flown in offended local pride and would have been an unacceptable call on the hosts' budget. So the British Guiana Board offered two new names: one, with the experience of standing in two previous Test matches, was coming out of retirement while the other, a newcomer to Test umpiring, was also head groundsman at the Bourda, where the match was being played.

It was the game in which England finally began to fight back in the series, led by a superb innings of 169 in almost eight hours of intense concentration, played by their captain Len Hutton. A final total of 435 was a strong one, and it looked even stronger when, after a tropical downpour, West Indies slumped to 139 for seven halfway through the fourth day of the six-day match.

Wicket-keeper Clifford McWatt, a local man, then joined the Jamaican Holt, who was batting down the order with a pulled leg muscle and, when the score had reached 237, they had added 98 runs. 'The crowd here,' Swanton wrote, 'has a habit of clapping softly and rhythmically when one or two runs are needed to reach a round figure. So the applause started and it rose to a crescendo as McWatt went for a second run that would have made 100.'

Alas, the next moments brought fresh disaster to the tour. 'It was a hazardous run, and a fast pick-up and throw to the top of the stumps by May enabled

Evans to run out McWatt by perhaps a couple of yards. McWatt, having seen the umpire's signal that he expected, just went on running to the pavilion.'

There was a brief, stunned lull. Then a bottle was hurled onto the field, soon followed by hundreds more. Crates, cans and all manner of other projectiles landed on the outfield. This was the tour's ugliest moment, but it came when England's priority was to press on and win a Test match. Despite advice to make for safety, Hutton and his team remained in the centre of the field, out of range of the bottles and determined not to leave. "We want another wicket or two," the captain is reported as saying.

Mr W.S. Jones, President of the British Guiana Board of Control, urges Len Hutton to lead his players off the field

Eventually, with the aid of the mounted police, the riot was contained and Laker bowled Ramadhin to give Hutton the wicket he was looking for.

"What we couldn't make out," says Charles, "was whether this trouble with the bottles was politically motivated or just people having too much rum and betting on whether the batsmen would reach their hundred. It was extraordinary what some of those boys would bet on if they'd had a rum or two; they'd bet a fortnight's wages. But we felt it was our job to ensure that, whatever happened, our players were protected. So we spoke to the Governor and said we would like the riot police brought in. He thought this over for a bit and then agreed that it was a good idea."

"Nowadays, with all the football riots there have been," Charles says, "it all pales into insignificance. But in those days it was quite outstanding to have something like that happen."

The umpire who gave McWatt run out was the groundsman, and throughout the rest day a police guard stood outside his house. News came through that, at the Queen's Park ground in Port-of-Spain in Trinidad, where the tourists were due next, two stands had been burnt down in an arson attack. But there was no more trouble in Guiana, and England - with a nine-wicket victory - brought the series back to 2-1.

The party then moved on via Grenada to Trinidad, where the match against the colony team gave Charles the chance to show his best batting form. His Leicestershire chairman, Frank Smith, had now joined the tour and he was able to see his county captain stroke a fluent 87 as MCC won by seven wickets.

The matches in Trinidad were played on jute matting, the Test ending as a high-scoring draw, with centuries by all three Ws as well as Compton and May. Unfortunately, once again the match was marred by several controversial umpiring decisions. Neither of the chosen officials, Ellis Achong, a former Test player, or his 24 year-old partner Ken Woods, had previously stood in a Test match.

The worst moment came off the last ball before lunch on the first day, with Achong standing at the end where Compton was bowling. According to EW Swanton, 'Holt chopped at a ball outside the off stump, and Graveney to all appearances made a comfortable waist-high catch at slip. Holt began to walk away, but apparently was struck by doubt, as presumably was the umpire, who answered the resultant appeal in his favour.'

'I could hardly believe my eyes,' Tom Graveney wrote later. 'For the first and I hope the last time, I lost my temper on the cricket field. I flung the ball down, called to Holt: "That's the fourth bloody time," and stalked off to lunch to the hissing and booing of the crowd.'

For the third time in the series the umpires lodged an official complaint about the behaviour of England players. It was not a happy state of affairs, but Alex Bannister recalls the reaction of Stuart Surridge, the combative captain of Surrey, who had come out to watch some of the cricket that winter. "At the end of the day he'd seen about four strange decisions and he said to me, 'How have they kept their sanity?'"

For the final Test the team returned to Jamaica for what was to prove the most remarkable match of the tour. Still two matches to one down, they needed to win. But, with Statham unfit to play and Laker still recovering from a blow to the face in the previous Test, the portents were not good.

"The pitch was bone hard like marble," Charles says. "You could see your reflection in it."

"Bat first, and you should make 700," the groundsman told Len Hutton.

"Our only hope was to bat," Trevor Bailey recalls, "then bowl them out with spinners. And Len lost the toss. I've never seen him more depressed."

Opening the attack in the absence of Statham, Bailey struck three times in the first half hour, finishing with seven for 34 as the West Indies managed only 139. "I was bowling at the wrong end," he says, "and everything went right. By evening I was going out to bat with Len."

"Three for 100 would have been really good figures on that," Charles says, "and Trevor took seven for 34. Then Len batted nine hours for his 200. He'd got such powers of concentration, and a wonderful technique. But Trevor, somehow he had produced something out of the bag which was quite impossible."

England batted through the second day and into the third – when, at the tea interval, Hutton had reached a chanceless 205, an innings that had EW Swanton glowing with admiration:

> One has been watching Hutton now for the best part of 20 years, and in that time he has built a record of achievement second only to Sir Donald Bradman's. Whatever he does, he has almost lost the capacity to surprise us. Yet from the viewpoint of physical stamina and mental concentration this latest innings is a thing apart, at any rate so far as the post-war years are concerned.

In reply to West Indies' 139, England had scored 392 for six, and Hutton's great effort had put his side on the verge of squaring the series. But any teatime euphoria was quickly dissipated when a large man burst into the team's dressing room, grabbed Charles by the lapels, lifted him off the floor and shook him. "This is the crowning insult," he said. "Your captain has insulted our prime minister."

As a first step towards greater self-rule the nationalist leader Alexander Bustamante had been appointed Jamaica's first Chief Minister, and he was at the pavilion gate when Hutton came off the field. "Len had batted for nine hours," Charles says, "and he came off for tea with just a few minutes to change and get back on the field. He had to get through all the people who wanted to slap him on the back and shake hands and all the rest of it. And unknown to me, and unbeknown to Len, Bustamante had decided that he was going to stand in the queue, because he was a big chap and the cameras could see him and they were pointing in that direction. Len just put his head down and went into the dressing room to have a cup of tea."

So it was that the diminutive Charles found himself in the vice-like grip of the largest member of the Chief Minister's entourage. "I said, 'Half a minute, put me down and we'll talk about it.' Then we had 48 hours of absolute non-stop political shenanigans, trying to say the right thing, which I think we did in the end. Len said, 'I'm not going to apologise.' Well, in the end he did. So it was a cat and mouse job as to what story was believed."

Hutton and Bustamante had a reconciliatory drink, and the Chief Minister made a statement that he had not been insulted. However, the local reporters preferred to play up the episode, and there were more unflattering headlines for the tourists to endure.

Almost everything had gone wrong for three months: from minor complaints by white people in the hotels to a major row with the Jamaican Chief Minister, from the felling of Headley to the no-balling of Lock, from umpiring disputes and riots to hostile articles in the local press. "Morning, noon and night something was happening," Charles recalls. "It got to the stage where I didn't know where the next arrow was coming from. All I knew was that it was coming."

The final Test, at least, had been played in a good spirit. There had been no fresh umpiring problems, and the goodwill between the two sides – so fractured at the start of the tour – seemed to have been restored. England won by nine wickets on the fifth day, and the series ended two-all. After three months of drama, there were no World Champions.

The squaring of the series was a personal triumph for Len Hutton, who had hit 677 runs at an average of 96.71. But back in England he missed most of the following summer and, after his 205 at Kingston, he played just 15 more Test innings and managed only 306 more runs. "Len reckoned that the West Indies tour shortened his career by two years," Charles says. "I'm surprised that he only said two. That innings in the fifth Test, he batted nine hours in the heat. After all the worries of the tour, he was magnificent."

After four months in the Caribbean heat the tourists sailed out of Kingston on the Stirling Castle. *The Times*, thinking back to the Bodyline tour 21 years earlier, called this West Indian trip 'the second most controversial tour in cricket history.' To *Wisden*, the primary intention of the tour, 'to further friendship between man and man, country and country', was not achieved.

"There was some marvellous cricket played," Charles reflects, "but, if you compare the tour with the enjoyment of the South African tour of '48, it was like chalk and cheese. I remember getting to the Equator on the boat and thinking, 'We're not far from home now,' and we perked up a bit."

CHAPTER 11

THE INQUEST

It was with a feeling of relief that Charles returned to England and the routine of county cricket, but he had not heard the last of the West Indies tour. Early in the summer he was summoned to Lord's to face the full MCC committee, and in a sometimes hostile atmosphere he was required to address criticisms of his management. "There were one or two people who made you feel that you had your head on the chopping block and they just wanted to see how the axe was going to be wielded."

Charles still preserves the letters from some of those present. Harry Altham, then Treasurer of MCC and newly appointed Chairman of the selectors, wrote to say, 'how admirable I thought you were when you came to Lord's for the difficult committee meeting.'

Another was from Gubby Allen, who had captained and managed the previous MCC tour to the West Indies:

> Dear Charlie,
> Just a line to congratulate you on a fine performance yesterday.
> You had to take a section of the committee which was, and I know what I am talking about, very hostile to the events of last winter and were looking for any slip on your part which would help their case. You were so very clear and forthright in your answers that they got absolutely nowhere.
> I am convinced that had Trueman not been a member of the team, that had you been given a different brief and more power, and that had Len been persuaded that a bloody battle did not necessarily involve a lack of courtesy, much of the trouble would not have occurred.
> Looking to the future now, I would like your opinion. Do you think a manager on a rather higher level is a solution and indeed a worthwhile proposition, especially if Len is to captain?
> Yours
> Gubby

"It was very heartening to receive those letters," Charles says. Yet he has never returned to West Indies, and his memories of that tour are the least happy of a lifetime in cricket that has given him so much pleasure. His pain has been the greater for having to bear so much criticism of his management, criticism that was led by the formidable EW Swanton.

It is difficult to understand how MCC came to choose as manager a man just 34 years of age with no first-hand knowledge of the Caribbean, to have given him no assistance, and then to have compromised his authority by expecting him as a player to be answerable to his captain. Swanton called it 'just about the worst decision ever to have come out of Lord's.' But, given such a very difficult assignment, what sort of job did Charles do?

Swanton's assessment of his performance is laid out in a letter written some two years after the tour and addressed to Lord Cobham, an influential figure at Lord's. He refers to Hutton's declared preference for Billy Griffith as manager as 'a proved success as a diplomat and disciplinarian' and continues:

> MCC sent Charles Palmer who made scarcely the slightest impact either on Len, or on the side, or on the West Indians. The result was a diplomatic and sporting disaster of the first magnitude which, I am sure, could have been averted by the right man.

"Oh, that's absolute rubbish," Alex Bannister, for 32 years cricket correspondent of the *Daily Mail*, says. "It's so wrong, so wrong."

Charles' own reaction to Swanton's missive betrays an uncharacteristic irritation: "He makes himself out to be Lord God Almighty all the time. 'What I say is right because I'm the only person who's got the right ideas about life and cricket. Everybody else is a bloody fool.' When I first met him, I thought, 'This is an impossible man.' There are times when I could have killed him – but times when I liked him!"

Charles recalls how, some time after he left Bromsgrove School, Swanton visited there. "He was carting this film around, on the 1950/51 tour of Australia. I asked the Headmaster how the visit had gone. 'It was a very good film;' he said, 'but I did occasionally get the impression that I was entertaining royalty.'

"He was the biggest snob of all time, and I couldn't get on with him at all. I think I hid it; I hope I did. But in later years, and especially after he married, he got mellower, and I realised that there was more to him than I thought. I think he was a very, very good writer. I think he loved the game – though, whether he loved the game more than he loved Swanton, I don't know!"

Alex Bannister agrees. "Later on, he was much more agreeable. And Bradman rated him the best cricket writer ever for his output and his knowledge of the game. But I must say, in West Indies his judgment was flawed. It was a very, very tough tour, particularly for Hutton and Palmer. I think they stood together marvellously well. They trusted each other. But for Palmer's clever and honest appraisal of every situation the tour wouldn't have made it."

Thirty years later Bannister would assist Hutton with his autobiography, *Fifty Years in Cricket*. "I knew Len very well," he says. "He used to come into my room at night and discuss what was going on. He would tell me things which perhaps I ought not to have been told. Len said that Charles couldn't have done better. I think it could be said without exaggeration that, if you hadn't had Charles Palmer about, that tour would have disintegrated into a real dog fight."

Swanton and Bannister. Rarely can two sports journalists have come to such different conclusions about the same events. "I thought Alex Bannister had a much more balanced view of the tour than Swanton," Charles says. "Swanton was always more concerned with who he had had dinner with the previous night."

Bannister recalls with amusement the attention Swanton paid to formal protocol wherever he toured: "In Australia, for instance, in each centre the governor had an open book in which when you arrived, if you so wished, you put your name down. And Swanton was always one to rush off and do that. What he got out of small talk with the Governor General of these places I wouldn't know."

In Swanton's view, the tour was a disaster, with the MCC party giving offence to both white and black West Indians and leaving behind so much ill-will that he returned two years later with his own privately raised tour party to repair some of the damage.

But Bannister, unlike Swanton, spent his time with the team and knew what they were having to endure. "We stayed in one hotel where I don't think my room had been dusted since it was built, and the bed was so poor that for the three weeks we were there I just sat on a chair and tried to sleep. I remember there was a mosquito net with holes big enough for a turkey to get in."

On their first visit to Jamaica they shared cramped rooms and were kept awake by the barking of dogs. So, when Charles was criticised for demanding that the West Indies Board find them something better for their return, Bannister's sympathies were with the manager. His own contribution to a more harmonious future for tours to the West Indies came when Sir Donald Bradman sought him out in advance of the Australian visit there the following winter.

"He told me that Ian Johnson was going to be captain and he said, 'Will you have a talk to him?' I spent two or three hours with Ian, telling him what the players should avoid doing and so on. He was very grateful to me and so was Bradman. They went prepared for the problems that existed in West Indies."

The Australians won the series three-nil, and they were popular wherever they went. 'We all enjoyed their tour very much,' Clyde Walcott wrote. 'On the field everything went smoothly, and there was hardly an incident worth the telling.'

Swanton and Bannister. The conclusions of their two tour books were very different. Swanton wrote:

> Mr Palmer is a charming, gentle person, whom to know is to like … but in his dealings both with his own players and with the various West Indian officials and governing bodies he was diffident in asserting himself.

Bannister wrote:

> Many wondered if Charles Palmer was a strong enough personality to be the manager of such a rumour-ridden and exacting tour, but he tackled a terribly difficult job with a quiet effectiveness which had to be admired.'

"Confrontation for confrontation's sake is anathema to me," Charles says. "I certainly am not one to bang the drum and say, 'Well I'm the boss.' We've had one or two of them in cricket! I suppose I could be accused of being too willing to agree with somebody unless it is something very specific that I feel very strongly about. I don't want to go through life having a bloody argument every few minutes."

"I remember several of us talking when we were out there," says Alex Bannister, "and we wondered what would have happened if, say, Freddie Brown or Wilf Wooller or any of that type of aggressive captain had been out there. I don't think it would have lasted to the half-way stage. There'd have been a real blinding bust up." Hutton himself, Bannister says, wondered what would have happened with Douglas Jardine calling the shots or if his own former Yorkshire skipper, the combative Brian Sellers, had been in charge.

Has MCC ever sent out a team on such a difficult tour with such an inadequate briefing and with only an inexperienced manager, doubling as player, to look after events? "One of my main gripes after the tour was that we were not adequately briefed either by the government or by MCC," Charles says. But he refutes any suggestion that he had no help from Lord's once they were in the Caribbean. "I couldn't have had more help or encouragement from Billy Griffith. If there was something I needed, he would have fallen over backwards to help. He was that sort of person." But this was an age before easy telecommunication and, in the words of Alex Bannister, Charles and Len Hutton "were two innocents abroad."

"I think Charles did a very good job in a very difficult situation," Tom Graveney says. "These days they've got assistant managers, coaches and God knows how many people helping out, but really Charles did almost all of the hard work."

"It was crazy to send a manager who hadn't been to the country before," Trevor Bailey says. "Typical MCC. Gubby Allen at his absolute worst, and his best wasn't very good. But Charles did the very best he could, and he's a delightful man, a very special person."

"I don't think I could have done very much more than I did," Charles himself reflects. "We fell over backwards to be conciliatory, to the extent that I was sometimes criticised for being too much so. Perhaps a different man, a Freddie Brown or a Brian Sellers, somebody who could bang the fist, might have made it better. But then they might have made it a damn sight worse."

CHAPTER 12

A DIFFICULT SUMMER

For Leicestershire, 1954 was to be a season of disappointments, but for Charles new horizons were opening up. While he was still in West Indies, MCC had approached the county inviting them to nominate their captain as a candidate for the England Selection Committee.

Addressing the county's Annual General Meeting, Chairman Neville Dowen told members that they had discussed the request but had decided that 'it would be better for the general public and the side that his name should not go forward.' The local press buzzed with rival views, but Leicestershire were understandably reluctant to lose their captain for at least six matches.

Notwithstanding the county's decision, MCC later availed themselves of Charles' services when they invited him, along with Norman Yardley, to augment the selection panel to choose the party to tour Australia. This same enlarged group was also responsible for the selection of MCC's team to play the touring Pakistanis and for choosing the Gentlemen and Players sides for the match which would give those with an eye on a winter tour an opportunity to show their paces.

The committee's first task was to choose a captain. Despite Len Hutton's success in West Indies, there were those who still believed that captaincy of a touring team sat uneasily on the shoulders of a professional. The problems of the previous winter and doubts about Hutton's health encouraged the media to make the most of any possible tussle for the captaincy between the incumbent and David Sheppard. Sheppard had captained Sussex with exceptional flair the previous summer, lifting his county from thirteenth to second in the Championship, and when Hutton was forced out of the second and third Tests against Pakistan, it was the young Sheppard to whom the selectors turned.

Sheppard himself was by now committed to a life in the church and was studying for ordination in Cambridge; but those who saw him as the man to retain the Ashes were determined that this should not be an obstacle. Sheppard later revealed that he had indeed been sounded out, with conspiratorial secrecy by MCC Secretary Ronnie Aird, and that, after consulting with the Principal of his theological college, they had concluded that it would be appropriate for him to tour if required as captain, but that he should not break his training if chosen purely as a player. It was not an easy situation for Sheppard to handle when the media were looking for a straight answer on his availability, and it helps to explain why the sub-committee minutes are silent on the whole captaincy issue apart from reports on Hutton's health.

The popular press did its best to nurture the controversy. And one Sunday afternoon there was a knock on the door at Charles' Leicester home. There on the doorstep stood Crawford White of the *News Chronicle*. "He was a bit of a smoothie," says Charles, "but I liked him in the end. He came here on a

Sunday when there was a Test match on at Trent Bridge. 'Hello, I haven't seen you for a long time. I just happened to be passing.' I said, 'Come in and have a cup of tea.' So he came in. It was obvious that all he wanted was to find out from me – is it Sheppard or Hutton? And he went all the way round the houses, questioning me for half an hour. I said, 'Drink your tea; it'll get cold.'

"He got it wrong anyway, but as he went out of the door – because I was as tight-lipped as I ought to be – he said, 'It is Hutton, isn't it?' I said, 'I don't know. You're the one who knows!' And he buzzed off without any information from me. But it would have been so easy in that half-hour to let loose the fact that I knew what the answer was, but I wasn't going to let him know."

After all the intervening years, Charles, the last survivor of those who made the decision, has no recollection of the matter going to the vote. And where did his own sympathies lie? "I went for Hutton for the simple reason that I'd lived with him through thick and thin in the West Indies. As far as I was concerned David Sheppard was a budding archbishop. I'd played a lot against him when he was at Cambridge, and he had hit 186 against us here, but I didn't know him well."

Had Charles found himself trying to persuade others of the merits of sticking with Hutton? "I didn't try to bring any positive influence to bear on it. The people who were the members of that committee were far more experienced in the ways of cricket than I was, when you think of Yardley, Robins, Wyatt and Harry Altham. From the point of view of knowing cricket and life they could have eaten six of me for breakfast."

But when it came to knowing Len Hutton might Charles not have pointed to rather more experience? "Well possibly," he concedes.

Later that summer Charles and his fellow selectors met to choose the full touring party. There were two inspired choices: "The two flyers we took were Tyson and Cowdrey." At the time the preference for Tyson over Trueman was controversial, but Charles supported it. "I'd certainly played against Tyson and I was happy to vote for him. At that stage Trueman was just a fast bowler with none of the guile that he learnt afterwards. Because Fred developed quite a good repertoire of guile."

A place was also found for Peter Loader, who had been brought into the Gentlemen and Players match, in the words of the press release, 'in place of AV Bedser because the MCC Selection Committee wish to see him in a representative match and feel he has earned his place on current form.' "Loader was more of one to bounce people out," Charles feels, "straightforward speed – and he was fast."

Had there been a vendetta against Fred Trueman? Charles thinks not; he believes that the fast bowling selections could all be defended on cricketing grounds. Nevertheless, among the many players whose names appear on the lists of those canvassed as to their availability by MCC, Trueman is a notable absentee. Moreover, he alone is afforded a special minute that suggests that, whatever the cricketing merits, there were those who would have preferred to keep him off the boat. As late as 14th July the feeling was that 'at present no letter on availability should be sent to FS Trueman. This, however, does not exclude FS Trueman from consideration for selection.'

The expanded selection panel: (from left) Gubby Allen, Walter Robins, Len Hutton, Harry Altham, Les Ames, Charles Palmer, Norman Yardley Bob Wyatt is absent from the photograph

Other contentious omissions from the party for Australia revolved around the spinners, where history has dealt less kindly with the selectors' choices. While Jim Laker was ignored, Robin Marlar had come into the reckoning – he was to be watched in the Gentlemen and Players match – before the Glamorgan off-spinner Jim McConnon was finally chosen to tour. "In Australia orthodox spinners had never done very well," Charles maintains in defence of this selection. "Laker and Lock were probably flatter, lower trajectory, but McConnon, if I remember rightly, was pretty tall and might have given it a bit of a loop. He had more variety in the air."

Tyson was the headline-grabbing hero of the tour and, with Colin Cowdrey also proving an inspired choice, the selectors could take some quiet credit when Hutton's men won the Ashes series 3-1. "We were accused of not knowing our business," Charles recalls, "but we had the last laugh!"

*　　*　　*

Charles had arrived home from the Caribbean in the second week of April, but he had little opportunity for rest as Leicestershire's first match was on 1st May. After the county's unprecedented success the previous year, it was a most disappointing summer: the coldest and gloomiest of the whole twentieth century. The county lost an average of almost five hours a match to the weather, and they plunged down the table from third to sixteenth.

In 1953 the team's success had been built around the performance of its all-rounders, but in 1954 it was a different story. In the county's annual Charles puts his finger on Leicestershire's problem: 'In the prevailing wet conditions our all-rounders did not measure up to the specialists. Of the all-rounders the batsmen were not good enough bowlers and the bowlers not good enough batsmen' He later adds: 'Our main batsmen are mostly stroke players who thrive *relative* to other batsmen on faster wickets.'

As one who always enjoyed playing his strokes, Charles himself was one of several key players who performed less well. Walsh, the only Leicestershire bowler to have taken a hundred wickets in a post-war season, missed the harder crumbling pitches of 1953, while Charles felt that neither Munden nor Jackson spun the ball sharply enough to take advantage of the softer wickets. When the faster bowlers were most needed to step into the breach, Goodwin lost form while Spencer was often away on National Service.

To compound their problems, there were no rising stars in the second eleven. In the words of MJK Smith, an Oxford undergraduate who played for the county in July and August, "they had nothing in reserve."

The county was trying hard to plug gaps with local talent, but Spencer and Boshier in the bowling department, Hallam as a batsman and Ray Julian, who would become the successor to Firth as wicket-keeper, were the only youngsters born within the county's boundaries to make the grade.

Charles' efforts to identify promising young players had begun as far back as his first winter in Leicester, when he had regularly visited the indoor cricket nets at Aylestone Road. Among those he felt might make a county cricketer was 16 year-old Freddie Foulds.

"My grandfather bought me twenty hours of individual coaching for eighty shillings," Freddie remembers. "I used to go to the indoor school. A wooden building with an old coke-burning stove in the dressing room. I can't remember if we had showers, I don't think so. There might not have been water laid on. But this open stove, I can remember. A wooden building with an open coal fire. You wouldn't get away with it today.

"The three coaches were Maurice Tompkin, Gerry Lester and George Geary. George Geary used to put a newspaper on the floor, and he used to bowl the ball on that newspaper all the time. And you'd be on-driving and off-driving. And Maurice Tompkin, he was so helpful, just super with everybody. But I always think it was Gerry Lester who got me into county cricket, and he also bowled me out of it because I could never play leggies – and Gerry was a big spinner of the ball."

By the spring of 1951 Freddie was one of five 16-year-olds taken onto the staff by Charles. "I think my salary was something like two and a half quid a week, and I can remember we got half a crown a day to go and buy our lunch at a café down the main road." Alas, he played only twice in the first team and, with John Davey and Peter Smith not establishing themselves either, the only two of the five recruits to stay long at the county were Bob Gardner, who scored 1,000 runs in 1959, and Mike Turner, who moved into the office and eventually became Chief Executive.

In Freddie's two first-class matches, he scored 1 and 0 against Cambridge University in 1952, then four years later he made a pair against Sussex. "I was sitting next to him in the dressing room," Charles recalls. "Just before he was going to go in to bat the second time. And I said, 'Now, Freddie, you're going to have a good day, aren't you? What would you really like today?' expecting him to say, 'Make fifty or a hundred." And he said, 'What I'd really like is a big bag of buns!'"

Another youngster, already on the staff, was Lol Spence. Taken on as a leg-spinner, he showed more promise as a batsman, though his first-class career was brief. "I didn't make the grade because I didn't have enough self-confidence. I was in awe of the senior players." He goes on to tell a story from the match against the 1953 Australians. "I fielded at short mid-wicket to Jack Walsh. He dropped one short to Neil Harvey, who was on about 60, and it was coming my way. There was a big crowd there, and I lost it. I put my hands up. Bang, in and out. Neil Harvey went on to make 200. Jack never spoke to me for quite some time after that."

Failing to establish himself as a player, Lol turned his hand to groundsmanship and in the 1970s he returned to Grace Road to give twenty years of service preparing pitches, earning the reward of a joint testimonial shared with Gordon Parsons in 1995. Throughout his time back at the club, Lol's shed was a popular meeting point for old cricketers wanting to exchange yarns.

"Gerry Lester was one. He used to sit and reminisce, go back and back. The groundsman's shed is a great place for that. When I was learning my trade at Wyggeston Boys' School, the groundsman was Bill Berridge, and this chap Frank Bale used to come and sit with him. They'd both played for the county in the 1920s, and they would talk for ever about the old days. You could sit there and listen to them for hours."

For many of these aspiring youngsters their dominant memories are of endless days as twelfth man for the first team and performing other duties around the ground. "I went on the field as twelfth man against Yorkshire at Sheffield," Freddie Foulds remembers, "and I fetched one from the boundary and attempted to underarm it back. But, instead of going forwards, it went over my head backwards. And when I eventually caught up with the skipper, Charles said, 'We're a cricket match here, not a circus.' I've used that phrase so many times in my cricketing life."

While still a schoolboy before joining the staff Freddie had been on the scoreboard for the match with the West Indians in 1950. "They were scoring so quickly, the board was never right all day. And we had to get up a ladder for the tens, not just the hundreds. So the ladder was permanently at the side of the board. Charles was shouting, 'Move the bloody ladder; we can't see the score.'"

"As twelfth man," says Lol Spence, "it was your job to get the kit together after the game, order the taxis to the station, see them all loaded on. Same the other end. Take it all to the ground, and then you'd go to the hotel. It was a nightmare really. And I think I was for ever being twelfth man."

"I was twelfth man at Hampshire," Mike Turner recalls, "and it was August Bank Holiday and, coming back, the guard's van was absolutely full of luggage, and I couldn't get these bags on until after midnight. I got back into Leicester at about four o'clock in the morning."

"We were playing Surrey," says Lol, "and the ground was under water. That's it, finish, no more play. But Stuart Surridge was captain of Surrey and he was very keen to play. So we had to get all the kit back. I'd ordered the taxis, and then they decided to play. Maurice Tompkin was furious. He had to get padded up, and he was out."

By the mid-fifties, Lol recalls that there were just enough cars for most of the team to make many of the journeys by road. "Jack Firth had an old clapped out Ford with a hole in the floor, and he had to put a brick under the back wheels."

"Then Malcolm Hickman came," Freddie adds. "He was a Casanova of the first degree. His father had got a bob or two, and he used to arrive in big flashy cars."

The twelfth men will not easily forget the weight of the leather bags, and Charles recalls the man, Mr Richards, who provided them. "Richards was a tartar of the old Victorian tub-thumping school. He used to give leather cricket bags – and they cost a lot of money in those days – to anyone who'd got his cap. And my script said: 'Now Mr Richards, do you want to be in the photograph of the presentation party?' 'No, I don't want any publicity whatsoever.' Then he'd be hanging around and I'd say, 'Oh, you'd better come in, Mr Richards.' 'Well, if you feel that way.'"

When his playing days ended, it was this same Mr Richards who would provide Charles with employment.

CHAPTER 13

SECRETARY AND CHAIRMAN

Winters at home provided Charles with little respite from the problems of the county club. Throughout his time as Secretary, Leicestershire's administrative affairs were conducted from two cramped rooms on the third floor of Spencer Chambers, 4 Market Place, in the city centre. Here Charles worked with a staff of two: Mrs Doore, his much-valued secretary, and Neville Stevens, a full-time book-keeper.

While the club had been awaiting Charles' arrival, Stevens had stood in as Secretary and Charles remembers him with great respect as an excellent worker, a man who made light of being severely crippled. "It must have been agony for him to have to climb up those three flights of stairs every day."

When Charles arrived at Leicester in the spring of 1950, he was reassured to know that at least the county could afford to offer him a three-year contract. But such was the success of his fund-raising initiatives that, by the summer of 1953, they were advertising for an Assistant Secretary – and the post was given to Tony Diment, who had played once for Gloucestershire the previous summer and who had moved to Leicester after marriage to work as a PE teacher in "probably the worst mixed secondary modern school in the city – it was dreadful." He arrived as Charles was leaving for the Caribbean.

Charles would not be back till three weeks before the season so he wrote out in long hand a list of all the things that needed to be done. Above the list, and recalling the help that he himself, as an inexperienced Secretary, had received from his counterparts at Edgbaston and Derby, he wrote a line of advice: 'If in doubt contact Leslie Deakins or Will Taylor.'

Heading the list was 'Hours of play', a matter where counties still had some individual latitude. 'Aim at 21 hours where practicable. Have a session with J Burbage about travel arrangements. Also get the players' angle from Lester, Tompkin or Jackson. See Wisden for regulations.'

There were notes on the meetings to be attended at Lord's and The Oval as well as the Leicestershire CCC committee meetings, normally held on the first Wednesday of each month, where agendas should be formulated with FSS (Frank Smith) and ONTS (Neville Stevens).

Then there was the AGM looming, where Tony should collaborate with Smith and Neville Dowen, checking the routine admin with Stevens. 'I will prepare minutes of the last meeting before I go,' Charles had written.

There were sub-committees on 'ground, finance etc', where Stevens and Mrs Doore would know the ropes and Tony was prompted to speak to someone at Roneo about printing requirements.

Players' terms and contracts would need to be followed up from the November meeting. The call-up date for the start of the pre-season practice should be agreed in consultation with Bill Ashdown.

Getting to know the office routine, understanding the accounts and the payment of salaries were ongoing tasks, to which were added a number of other matters that demanded Tony's attention. In later decades there would be a sharper commercial focus to the Secretary's responsibilities; now it was more a matter of keeping the show on the road with 'publicity and advertising' way down the list.

The headline tasks were:

- keeping an eye on the indoor school
- ordering the season's cricket balls
- getting the scoreboard fixed so that the overs could be displayed
- sorting out a regular scorer
- liaising with Bill Ashdown about new nets
- Tompkin's benefit
- talking to people at the Education Committee about the use of the Grace Road ground
- administration of the out-grounds and getting permission for their use through specific committee members
- arranging Second Eleven and Club and Ground matches with John Josephs
- working with ST Hickling and Jim Burbage on Leicester Youth Cricket Council
- preparing notes on the 1953 season for *Wisden* and *Playfair*
- getting the Year Book together
- getting the fixture cards printed
- distributing season tickets
- looking ahead to the 1955 fixtures
- catering
- reviewing the Pluvius insurance

Tony was also to work with Vic Jackson on players' hotel accommodation. Here there was some doubt as to what might now be required. The booking of hotels had been a task that Vic Jackson had looked after in the winter, with players paying their own board, but for 1954 the committee had decided 'to give a season's trial to the system whereby the Club arrange hotel accommodation for the players and pay the consolidated account presented by the hotel, on condition that the these accounts only include bed, breakfast and dinner, and lunch and tea on Sundays for week-end away matches.' By the middle of the next summer the terms would be amended to include morning tea for the players.

The book includes pages of calculations in Charles' handwriting with travel plans for journeys the team might need to make in the forthcoming season. If all went well, he hoped the team would arrive at Portsmouth at 11.22 pm, while for the Kent match they ought to reach Canterbury at 12.16 am. But the most gruelling journey of all read:

Ashby to Leicester by train or coach
Depart Leicester 5.55   Arrive Birmingham 7.00
Depart Birmingham 8.10   Arrive Hereford 10.14
Depart Hereford 10.40   Arrive Cardiff 12.35

"You more or less submitted your own plan of which grounds you were using for your home matches," Tony Diment remembers. "With not being able to use Grace Road much until August, we had to negotiate with Hinckley or Loughborough or Coalville or Ashby-de-la-Zouch to see whether they could accommodate us on the dates we wanted. And we'd try to get a week there if we could, because we had to transport everything out there."

As Secretary and Assistant for four years, Tony and Charles developed a harmonious working relationship. "Charles was a good organiser and, if he had confidence in you, he was happy to delegate. And he delegated well. But overall, I think he was still keeping an eye on things without your being a hundred percent aware of this. It's a great art, to delegate but not interfere, which Charles seemed to have the knack of doing. But I've no doubt he knew exactly what was going on all the time."

Charles and Tony would share the many evening commitments, setting off on the round of local cricket clubs, where they kept the flag flying for the county and stoked up interest in the football competition that was so vital to the club's financial well-being. "We would often leave the office at about half past four and have a game of squash. Then we'd both be on parade at a dinner somewhere, making a speech about the club. Charles was a very delicate squash player. All touch, very quick around the court, but not thrash bang. It was all delicate touches, angles and things. Typical Charles, really!"

Tony still plays golf, though Charles has now retired. "I remember him telling me, 'I've given up now. I've got to the stage where, if I'm in a bunker, I can get the ball out but I can't get myself out!'"

"Tony was a good golfer," Charles says. "He got down to a handicap of about six. We were playing together in a four-ball, a reasonably friendly one, and at one point he hit his second shot straight down the hole. We all said, 'Good shot, Tony'. We duly got up to the green and found he'd played my ball. And I've never let him forget it."

Charles found that committee members would lend a hand when there were special jobs to be done. However, their interest in affairs was not always a blessing. "We had one very nice old chap, who was retired and who had damn all else to do but come in and interrupt me in the middle of the morning. But, to get to my office, he had to come through the general office. So I would hear this bloke coming up. 'Is Mr Palmer in?' 'Yes.' And I'd be thinking, 'I'm stuck here for three quarters of an hour.' So I had the wall taken down and another door put in my office so that, when I heard him coming, I'd nip downstairs. There was a nice little café in the street, where I'd go and have a cup of coffee, and come back half an hour later. It saved me a lot of time."

There was always the chance for young professionals to earn a bob or two doing menial tasks, and among those given work in the office was Mike Turner. "When I was a boy I used to have some temporary work in the office, and there was another chap called Eddie Phillips. Charles used to get us to stuff envelopes and all those sorts of things. I remember there was a storage heater at one end of the committee room, and we used to play with these airflow cricket balls which, if you covered one side with Sellotape, you could make swing one way or the other. At lunchtime Eddie and I used to play in the committee room with the storage heater as the wicket, bowling in-swingers and out-swingers. Underneath was a firm of chartered accountants, and periodically someone would come up and say, would we mind not banging the bat on the floor."

At the end of 1957, Charles stepped down as Administrative Secretary, taking on instead the unpaid post of Honorary Secretary. He was replaced by Tony Diment, whose position as Assistant was shortly afterwards offered to Mike Turner.

"Happily I realised my own limitations as a player," Mike now reflects. He would still make occasional appearances for the county team, "but, when I went into the office, I played as an amateur. I remember playing at The Oval, and Lockie came into our dressing room, took my bag and put it in the old amateurs' room."

Charles, unusually for the time, arranged for the new Assistant to go on day release to the local College of Technology to study accountancy, economics and company law. "It was far sighted," Mike says, "and I remember Charles saying, 'At least we've got the chance of bringing you up the way we want you.'"

Then, after only two years in post, Tony Diment moved on and Mike Turner, at the age of 25, found himself appointed Secretary, in which position – later renamed Chief Executive – he stayed for 33 years.

Mike and Charles would forge one of the strongest partnerships in the county game, with both of them realising the need to have a strong grasp of commercial realities. The club's long-serving President Mr S.H.B. Livingston, a generous benefactor in his time, was now a sick man – "He had lost the ability to be of any assistance to us," remembers Charles, "and I was charged with the task of telling him to buzz off." – and in his place came Bill Bentley of Bentley Engineering, who quickly made clear what kind of man he was. "I am accustomed to being associated with success," he told Mike Turner.

The chairmanship, meanwhile, was in the safe hands of Neville Dowen, who had taken over on Frank Smith's death in 1956. "Our greatest friend," says Barbara. "He was a lovely chap," Charles agrees. "I remember one time he came down to Lord's, and he took Brian Chapman the reporter and me out to dinner at a place in Soho. He'd just discovered Chateauneuf du Pape, which you could then buy from an off licence for nineteen shillings a bottle, and he plied us with a very nice meal and he kept pouring this wine into my glass. And I said, 'No more, please. I've got to bat tomorrow.' Anyway I had another one, certainly more than I thought I should. But next day I got a hundred!"

Neville Dowen

Then in the autumn of 1964, following the death of Dowen, the chairmanship again fell vacant, and Charles was persuaded to take it on.

Tony Diment, from his spell as Secretary, knew how important the role of Chairman was. "The trouble with committeemen," he says, "is that they may all be high-powered in their own businesses, but they leave their brains in their cars. I remember back in the '50s, the majority of the committee would withdraw to The Saracen's Head for a drink afterwards, and in those days we had representatives for all the out-grounds as well, all these hosiery manufacturers running their own businesses. And I'd be standing there listening to their conversation, thinking, 'There's more sense being talked in this pub than there was in the committee room. Why didn't you say that in committee?'"

"Charles and I had a really nice relationship," Mike Turner says. "It was only after he retired that I had difficulties with people telling me how to run the club. Charles is quite a character, but he's not remotely confrontational. It's easy to work with him because you don't get involved in silly rows and things don't get built up out of perspective. The other thing was that he was so diplomatic. It was part of his make-up. I can't see him offending anyone."

"I think Mike enjoyed his time with me," Charles says, "in the sense that I didn't tread on his toes all the time a) because I didn't want to and b) because it was not necessary."

Charles put a premium on planning ahead of meetings. "Bill Bentley, Mike Turner and I used to have an hour together before the meeting started. So we knew what we wanted. And we were able sometimes to bulldoze things through. I could never take a committee meeting unless they stuck to the point. There was one chap who did a lot towards raising money from the football competition. But he could waffle, waffle, waffle. I'd say, 'Look I'll take that under any other business, but I'm not going to take it now.'"

"We had a working agenda," says Mike Turner. "We'd go to a meeting and perhaps something contentious would come up and Charles would talk for ten minutes or whatever, and there were times when we'd finished with the subject and moved on and it was going through my mind, 'I wonder what Charles really believes.' The committee had accepted what he'd said, yet he'd addressed both sides. He was so skilful, so diplomatic in the way that he dealt with people all the time."

From 1964 to 1989 they worked in tandem as Chairman and Secretary, and they were years of great progress. With the county still benefiting from its football pool competition, they converted the open stand into what is now

The Meet and in January 1966 purchased the ground from the Local Education Authority. Then came a new pavilion, bringing the club's offices into the ground.

Charles was aware that Leicestershire, as one of the smaller counties, had to find players from outside its boundaries. "Leicestershire's a tiny county, 600,000 people – fewer than that in those days – with a catchment area about a twentieth the size of Yorkshire, so we had to seek recruitment from outside."

For the 1965 season Turner lured Tony Lock from Australia and in 1967, in the second of Lock's two summers as captain, he led the county to equal second place in the championship. Then, when Ray Illingworth turned his back on Yorkshire at the end of 1968, an offer of the captaincy brought him to Grace Road. The same summer, after the relaxation of qualifying rules for overseas players, the Australian pace bowler Graham McKenzie was signed. "Mike Turner was a very good operator," Charles says. "He set out his stall to get good people."

No longer were Leicestershire the Cinderellas of county cricket, and at the end of the summer of 1975 they were raising the Championship pennant at the ground.

When Charles first envisaged Mike Turner as an administrator, he had been a leg-break bowler unable to make it into the county side, an ex-grammar school boy who had been willing to help out in the office and who was considering a more secure career with Michelin Tyres in Stoke-on-Trent. Now he was one of the most innovative and successful secretaries in English county cricket.

"I was the youngest ever when I took over," Mike says, "and I think Charles and the committee took a tremendous risk, for which I shall be eternally grateful."

"He didn't look the sort of chap who was going to fall into a big hole," Charles says, "but we thought, if he does, there's enough of us around to yank him out of it. Happily we never needed to do that."

CHAPTER 14

WHO'S GOING TO BOWL?

In the summer of 1955 Leicestershire bounced back to sixth in the championship table, winning eleven matches and losing ten. Maurice Tompkin scored 2,000 runs for the only time in his career, and Charles had a much better season, his 1,857 runs an increase of more than 600 on the previous year. In the Gentlemen versus Players match at Lord's, the two of them were the outstanding performers, Tompkin making 115 in the Players' first innings and Charles replying with 154 for the Gentlemen.

"Maurice was in his nineties and very anxious to get his first hundred in a Gents-Players match," Charles remembers. "I was bowling and I said to him, 'Third ball next over.' I was going to give him a juicy half-volley or something. And he said, 'OK, skipper.' He was so keen to hit it. His eyes popped out of his head, and he was going to bang it away. And he as near as dammit holed out at mid on. Thank God he didn't. The fielder missed it, and it ran away for his hundred."

Maurice Tompkin's fluent century helped to secure him a place on MCC's 'A' tour of Pakistan that winter, but he did not have the happiest of tours and was a sick man by the following summer. Little could either of them have realised but, when he hit Charles' friendly delivery for four at Lord's, it was the last time he would pass a hundred in a first-class match.

The summer of 1955 was one in which Charles made quite a name for himself as a bowler. In all matches that year, he took 48 wickets at an average of only 19.04 runs each. Though he always refused to take his bowling as seriously as his batting, he was an exceptionally economical bowler and one who brought useful variety to the Leicestershire attack.

Charles describes himself as "military medium", and those who played with him agree. "He was slow medium, not fast medium or anything like that," Terry Spencer says. "Accuracy was his main thing, off five or six paces. He broke a few stands for us: if you were a bit stuck for a wicket, he'd come on and maybe get you one. Perhaps there were times when he should have turned his arm over and didn't."

"He was a nice steady seam bowler, just medium pace," says Reg Simpson. "Some of the spinners get near to his pace nowadays. But there used to be quite a few bowlers of Charles' pace, people like Bertie Buse of Somerset – he was very difficult to play, he used to move the ball both ways on a good length, and you had to do all the work as a batsman. There were quite a few around, and you really had to bat to play them."

"There's not too many of Charles' pace in the modern game," Terry Spencer feels, "I can't think of any." "He was slow medium or medium medium," says Micky Stewart, citing Paul Collingwood as the closest to his type today. "But Charles had less pace than him. Paul Collingwood is more aggressive. He is trying to hit the pitch harder, but Charles would only kiss it."

But was Charles quite as slow as he seemed? Terry Spencer agrees with Tony Diment, who says: "What people don't realise is that he was a good yard quicker than he looked. He just used to amble up and throw his arm over, but he came off the wicket a good yard quicker than you expected. And I think that's where the deception came in."

Jack Firth, writing in 1954, saw him in a similar light. 'It would surprise most of the people who have not actually batted or kept wicket to his bowling, at the amount of pace he can get from a pitch helping him a little. I can remember occasions when this has happened, or when the ball has lifted sharply, and I have registered some surprise, he thinking it a great joke and saying, "I'll have you stood back before we're through!"'

Charles had bowled off-spinners at Old Hill, and up to 1951 the *Playfair Cricket Annual* listed him as a 'useful swing and OB bowler'. Then, after he had moved to Leicester, he was re-classified as 'accurate RM'. "He bowled a few cutters, but mostly seam," says Terry Spencer.

And, with this style of bowling, on Saturday 21st May he produced one of the most extraordinary performances in the whole history of first-class cricket.

The early weeks of the season had been damp and cold, and on that Saturday morning the visitors to Grace Road were champion county Surrey, who had already won their first five matches. Jack Walsh had chosen the match for his benefit and when, going out in place of Charles, he won the toss, Leicestershire opted to bat first.

Alas, little went right from this point and by tea-time they were all out for 114, with the mighty Surrey already 42 for one in reply. There had been an early wicket for Spencer, but Peter May was striking the ball with commanding ease.

The pitch had now dried out except for one spot. "The covers weren't great in those days," Terry Spencer explains, "and there was this wet patch about the size of a dinner plate." The two finger spinners, Jackson and Munden were bowling, and they approached Charles during the interval. "We're bowling at the wrong ends," they said, fancying that Jackson's off-spinners might make more of the damp spot. "Fine, I'll change you round," said Charles.

"It was only as we were walking out after tea that I suddenly thought, 'Oh heck, who's going to bowl this one over?' I might as well do it myself." This was Charles' sixth match of the summer, and he had bowled only four overs. He had never regarded himself as much more than an occasional bowler, and now, suffering from back trouble, his doctor had advised him against bowling at all. "'Oh well,' I thought. 'One over won't hurt me.'"

"Go easy on me," he said to Peter May. "I haven't bowled this year." He measured out his run and prepared to bowl a containing straight over. With his second ball he clean bowled the best batsman in England. "Back or no back, I had to continue then, didn't I?"

The fourth ball of his next over saw Bernie Constable caught by Gerry Lester from a skier, then the young Micky Stewart was bowled first ball for a

117

duck. "I just bowled straight," Charles claims.

Charles' accuracy meant that he was striking the wet patch with great consistency, and each time the ball hit the spot it appeared to hasten on. "Of course he was very accurate," says Jeff Goodwin, "but it was the skid that did it. He hit that little patch every time. It takes some doing, you know, but he did it." According to *The Times*, 'His medium pace swingers whipped viciously into the batsmen.'

In his fifth over Charles bowled Fletcher, the opening bat. The next over saw the end of Ron Pratt, bowled again, and he had figures of five wickets for no run. "He just treated it as a joke," Terry Spencer recalls. "After each wicket, he would say, 'I suppose I'd better have another over now.'" He had not conceded a run, and his team – enjoying the fun – fielded with tigerish determination. His eighth over brought him two more wickets: McIntyre and Surridge, both bowled. His figures now were seven wickets for no runs. After two more maidens, he bowled Tony Lock. Surrey were now 67 for nine, and his bowling analysis read: 11 – 11 – 0 – 8.

Wisden's list of Remarkable Analyses showed no complete analysis with a bowler having taken more than five wickets without conceding a run. Of those who had taken eight, the meanest return was Jim Laker's for just two runs, in the Test Trial at Bradford in 1950. 'Next to me,' wrote Crusader in the *Leicester Evening Mail*, 'someone muttered between his teeth, "I just pray he won't bowl any more. There's bound to be a run against him."' In the pavilion Jeff Goodwin, not in the team for the match, remembers Chairman Neville Dowen saying, "For Christ's sake, don't bowl again. You've got a world record that will never be beaten!"

Laker himself was now at the crease with Alec Bedser for company, and they each survived a maiden over. Terry Spencer, bowling from the far end, was at his most testing, but Laker then managed to take a single off him so that he was facing as Charles began his thirteenth over. The Leicestershire captain's figures stood at 12 – 12 – 0 – 8, but now the spell was broken.

"Jim took to smearing me," says Charles. "He hit a two that lobbed into the gap between cover and extra cover, then a two that went off an edge down to fine leg. Then there was a three. So I finished up with eight for seven. It could so easily have been nine for nil."

And what of the one that ballooned into the covers? Maurice Tompkin and Vic Munden were both in the vicinity of the ball. "But we couldn't have caught it," says Vic, "even if someone had dived."

Eventually Terry Spencer bowled Jim Laker for 14, Surrey were all out for 77 and the Leicestershire players formed a guard of honour for Charles as they left the field. Years later he still regards his 90-minute spell as one of life's oddities, the sort of extraordinary freak that the game loves to throw up from time to time. "According to my wife," he now says, "Peter May said that I went into the Surrey dressing room, opened the door and said, 'Gentlemen, I do beg your pardon.'"

Charles Palmer leads off the Leicestershire players
while a young autograph hunter approaches Alec Bedser

His explanations to the press were no less disarming. "I found my off-cutters turning about two inches, but the Surrey batsmen kept playing down the wrong line," he told reporters. "In fact, I bowled down the Metropolitan Line and they played down the Bakerloo." He wouldn't be taking up bowling again, Charles insisted. 'He doesn't even contemplate bowling in the second innings,' reported Peter Lorenzo in the *Daily Herald*.

That evening the celebrations got under way. "The only thing it taught me," he now says, "was how much whisky I could drink. And I think that I found out the answer very quickly."

Leicestershire's batting was soon faltering a second time and, despite half-centuries for Charles and Tompkin, there was only a modest target for Surrey on the second day, enabling May, Clark and Constable to take them to a seven-wicket win. And, when Charles bowled again, it was not until the fifth ball of his twelfth over that he conceded his first and only run in a spell of 13 overs. It left him with match figures that read: 27 – 24 – 8 – 8.

Letters of congratulation poured in. There were several friendly jibes about Charles' supposed lumbago problems. 'Not bad for one who stated within the last week that he had given up bowling!' wrote Kent Secretary Neville Christopherson. But the message that Charles treasures most, for its economy of words, came from a Worcestershire vicarage, where his former headmaster at Bromsgrove was now the incumbent. The post card from the Reverend David Walters read: 'Good show!'

Charles shows the ball to Tim and Andrew

The rest of the season had its highs and lows with several close finishes, none more exciting than when Yorkshire won by two wickets at Grace Road in early August. This was only the third time Tony Diment, Assistant Secretary and Second Eleven captain, had played for the first team and he made a good impression with scores of 48 and 47. "He hit the ball well if it was pitched up to him," Charles says. "But he got in a tangle when the quickies were up against him because, in the good old amateur fashion, he put his left leg down the wicket first and then suddenly he found he didn't ought to have done that!"

Tony's promotion into the first team allowed him to see Charles' leadership style at first hand. "He skippered the side in his schoolmasterish way, if you know what I mean. Quietly efficient, I would say."

Tony soon learnt that Charles was a stickler for the game's proprieties. "We were playing against Sussex at Grace Road on a turning wicket. Robin Marlar was bowling, and I was right on my back foot. The ball hit my glove and was caught by, of all people, David Sheppard at short leg. And before I could get back into my balance and walk, the umpire said 'Not out'. I was out about two overs later and, when I came in, Charles said to me, 'Were you out?' And I said, 'Yes'. He said, 'Well, when they come off the field, you can go into their dressing room and apologise to Robin Marlar.'

"And I had to go in and say, 'Sorry, Robin, I was out.' It was all done very quietly, but with a certain amount of authority behind it. I will never forget the humbling experience of having to go into that dressing room and apologise to Robin Marlar for not walking. I wasn't experienced enough to know what to do when the umpire had said 'Not out'."

Tony had learnt what lay behind Charles' mild-mannered exterior. "He was a *very* strong captain. He knew exactly what he was doing. I think some of the spectators thought he wasn't a good captain, but in fact he was a *very* good captain. He wasn't demonstrative and it was all done very quietly, but with a little bit of authority behind the whole thing."

For Charles, the interests of the team were always more important than those of the individual. "A couple of years later," Tony Diment recalls, "we were playing Sussex at Hove. We were all out for under 200, and I was top scorer with 67. I thought, 'Saturday night in Brighton, out with the lads, have a few beers.' And Charles said quietly to me, 'You're coming out and having dinner with me tonight.' And for three hours he talked to me and he said, 'It was your duty, as you were obviously the only one in form, to stay there and get a hundred for your side.'

"I don't think any of the other players knew about this at all, but he made his point that I had let the side down, even though I was top scorer. This was a side of him that a lot of people never saw. I can appreciate his feelings. I was inexperienced, and I was happily hitting Don Smith back over his head and thinking, 'This is great.' But I was being selfish, playing for myself."

But the game that Leicestershire most enjoyed winning that year was at Cardiff against Wilf Wooller's Glamorgan side. "Wilf Wooller could be very difficult," Tony Diment says. "And Haydn Davies, the wicket-keeper, could be difficult, too. We always seemed to have a bad game against Glamorgan."

Their problems started on the Friday evening when they arrived late at their hotel. "We got there at half past one in the morning," Jeff Goodwin says, "and we rang the bell. We kept on ringing, and finally someone came to the door. And, since we had been booked to stay there, the hotel had changed hands, and the people hadn't got a clue that we were coming. And there we were, a cricket team, at half past one in the morning. 'Who are you?' Well, Charles wasn't best pleased with that, because some of us had to sleep on mattresses on the floor. Next day we lost the toss and we were in the field."

Nor was Charles in a more conciliatory mood when the hotel served up Sunday lunch. "We all sat round this big table in this hotel. And afterwards Charles said, 'Could I have a word with the chef, please.' The waiter said, 'Yes, sir.' The chef came in and Charles said, 'That's the worst bloody meal I've ever had.' Oh, he didn't mince words at times."

The match went no more smoothly. "Haydn Davies appealed for a catch against Vic Jackson," Tony Diment remembers. "It was given not out, and he went on to make a hundred. That was on the Monday, and it went on and on, the chuntering about it. We had had to go to something that evening for somebody's benefit, and it was going on then. Haydn was still chuntering that Vic had been caught out.

"Tuesday lunchtime, I was sitting at the same table for lunch with Wilf and Charles, and it was still going on. And Charles said, 'Look, Wilf, if you don't stop this chuntering, I shan't take my team out after lunch. I've had enough of this.'

"It got to the stage where we needed 51 runs to win. And, as our opening pair Mike Smith and Gerry Lester went out to bat, Charles said, "If you knock these runs off and we don't lose a wicket, we shall have some champagne on the train going back to London. And I've never seen two more determined batsmen go out; and they knocked those runs off and we did have champagne on the train."

CHAPTER 15

PURE DONKEY DROPPINGS

Charles had taken Leicestershire to new heights, finishing in the top six three times in the four years from 1952 where in 47 previous summers they had managed it only twice. But he had achieved this with an ageing side, and by 1956 there was an urgent need for fresh talent. Jack Walsh was 43, Gerry Lester 40, Vic Jackson 39, and all three would fade away over the next two summers.

In Jeff Goodwin's memory there had always been an elderly feel to the side. "That's why they all wanted to field in the slips. 'I'll go in the slips, skipper.'"

Worse was the decline of Maurice Tompkin, whose stylish batting had been a vital component of the county's success and who in 1956 managed just 635 runs at an average of 18. "I know he complained about his back," Jeff says, "and he was told it was lumbago, coming from a hot climate to a very cold one, and that he'd be all right. He was still playing at the beginning of September, and by the end of the month we were burying him."

"It hit us very hard," says Charles. "They found he he'd got cancer. He was only 37."

The loss of Tompkin was compounded by the inability of the Yorkshireman Gerry Smithson to score the runs expected from him. "He was a great stroke player," says Charles, "but he didn't harness his talents completely. He wasn't quite the old Yorkshire 1930s stamp. But I do remember one occasion when he was going in first and, for some reason, he got mixed up as to whether it was the first or second bell. Anyway, he had to wait and he went in in a raging temper. Why, God only knows. He only had to wait ten minutes, but I suppose his adrenalin had been raised and I can't remember if he got a hundred before lunch, but if he didn't he ought to have done. He hit everybody all over the ground."

To add to Leicestershire's troubles, Mike Smith, earmarked as Charles' successor, decided before the start of 1956 that his future lay with Warwickshire. "I'd started to get a bit of a taste for the game," he says, "and I decided that I'd probably go into cricket administration. I went over to Edgbaston because it was a Test match ground." "We'd like to have kept him," says Charles, without rancour.

Other young players were unable to fill the vacancies left by Walsh, Jackson and Tompkin. Maurice Hallam began to emerge as a high-scoring opening batsman, but Vic Munden was never as effective, once he became the number one spinner. "Vic was a very useful cricketer," says Mike Smith, "but he didn't move up from behind Jackson and Walsh. Because the time comes when you've got to do a man's job."

John Savage and Jack van Geloven were two bowlers who began to emerge. At the end of 1956 it fell to Savage to bowl the last ball of the season to Worcestershire's number eleven batsman Aldridge. A wicket would lift

Leicestershire off bottom place in the table but, alas, with all the fielders clustered around the bat, the ball was played away safely. The following summer Savage was the county's leading bowler, but again they finished bottom, now 32 points below Worcestershire in sixteenth place and with only two victories.

Jack van Geloven, a Yorkshireman, took longer to emerge, but in 1962 he became the fifth and last Leicestershire player to complete the double. "He was a great trier," Charles says. "If you put him on into the wind he'd bowl into the wind. He'd try and try and try, and he'd never complain. But he wasn't blessed with much up top. I remember he was going to South Africa for a coaching job. We were going down to Portsmouth on the train and, before we got there, he came up to me and said, 'Skipper, can you help me?' I said, 'Of course if I can.' He said, 'I've got this bit of paper here and I don't understand it.' I had a look at it, and I said, 'Turn it over. That's the Afrikaans side.'"

With no experienced spinners, the quicker bowlers had a more important part to play. Brian Boshier made few appearances in 1956, but Jeff Goodwin had one of his better years as Terry Spencer's opening partner. There had once been great hopes for Spencer, and in 1953 he had played in the Test trial, taking the wickets of Bailey, Compton, May and Simpson while at the other end Aircraftsman Trueman went wicketless. 'With a high, easy action,' *Wisden* reported, 'he made the ball move off the seam and extracted more life from slow turf than some of the faster bowlers.'

"What interfered with my career was the two years National Service," he says.

"Everybody in the Army looked upon him as a fast bowler," Charles says, "and he tried to be a fast bowler, but he was really a fast-medium bowler. He frightened one or two people so he tried to be a fast bowler even more. He was a bit wild to start with. We were playing Derbyshire at Burton, when Gladwin and Jackson were there, and it was a wicket where each ball made a mark; it was damp enough for that. I said 'Terry, you're all over the place. I'll show you where your balls are landing; and you can see this is Gladwin and Jackson.' Their marks were all within a dinner plate size."

The weakness of the county's bowling meant that Charles now bowled more. In 1956, for the first and only time, he sent down more than 500 overs, and his 50 Championship wickets came at 16.48 each. Notwithstanding his day of glory against Surrey, Charles had always regarded himself as a part-time bowler. But now he added a new delivery to his armoury: the lob or 'donkey drop'.

It all began at Grace Road in the traditional Whitsun derby against Northants, then one of the stronger counties. "Bank Holiday games were the main highlights of the county season," Charles says, "and our rivalry with Northamptonshire attracted the fiercest local patriotism. They had Jock Livingston, the fine Australian left-hander; he always had great success against us, and that day he looked set for another big score. And heaven knows why, but I was bowling to him. I ran in from the pavilion end, and to this day I have no idea what motivated me to throw the ball right up in the air. I took a run of only ten short paces, and certainly at the beginning of my run-up I had no idea of bowling a 'donkey drop'."

Mike Turner was one of the young players on the ground: "You could see Jock Livingston winding up, but this donkey drop was absolutely perfect. It went up and up and up. At first Jock thought he was going to be able to hit it over here, then he was going to hit it over there. And it ran off the blade of his bat and Maurice Hallam caught it at first slip." The annual report described Livingston's shot as 'like a Highlander tossing the caber.'

"A few days later," Charles says, "I received by post a small parcel containing a cigar which had been re-wrapped, with a band inscribed 'Guaranteed made of pure donkey droppings'."

Another victim was Kent's Bob Wilson at Gravesend the following May. "I'd seen off Spencer and one or two of the others," the left-handed Wilson recalls, "and I'd reached 157. After I'd got my 150 I'd doffed my cap and taken the applause and thought that I would sail on and see if I could get to 200, which I never did and always wished I could have done.

"Charles came on to bowl and, although I'd heard he was capable of bowling this particular type of ball, I didn't think I would be the subject of one of them as I was well in. But I can still remember Charles with his little jaunty run-up. He only ran a few paces and he let this ball go. And up it went and I stood transfixed at the other end. And it kept going and it then started to descend behind me, and I was reluctant to let it go and as it dropped behind me I turned in the crease, swung my bat thinking it was going to go for four and I missed it and knocked all three out."

Livingston and Wilson were in good company. When the West Indians visited Grace Road in 1957, Asgarali, Kanhai and Worrell all fell to Palmer donkey drops, the first two to catches by Diment and Spencer and Worrell, with a century to his name, another hit wicket victim.

Terry Spencer remembers holding a few catches off Charles' lobs. "The best bats in the country didn't know what to do. It came up behind them and dropped on the stumps. They didn't know whether to hit now or pull it later, and I caught two or three at mid-wicket when they mishit it."

Mike Turner remembers how Terry would react when he saw the donkey drop leaving Charles' hand. "Terry used to field at short leg and as soon as he saw it go he immediately retreated to the square leg area. I can see it in my mind's eye, Terry retreating and straight down his throat."

This is exactly how another victim, Tom Cartwright, recalls it: "I'd never seen it before. And suddenly he arrived at the crease and lobbed it up. It wasn't just a bit higher than this ceiling. It was miles up, and it was so accurate. It came down right on top of you. And you didn't know whether to leave it or what to do. You couldn't head it. In fact, I was quite pleased when I hit it. I hit it quite hard, quite well. But Terry Spencer, who'd been at leg slip, as soon as it had gone up, ran a long way to backward square leg and I hit it straight at him."

Embarrassment, laughter and unexpected wickets, the donkey drops certainly added to the day's entertainment. But they were also balls of consummate skill. Charles explains the recipe: "The success of this type of ball depends on several things. It must be high enough for a steep descent, at least 30 feet, or it will merely be a full toss. It must be straight; it must be full enough length to land on or very near the stumps if missed. And it must be used sparingly enough to be something of a surprise to the batsman. The one I bowled to Jock Livingston met all four requirements but, since it was my first ever, perhaps the element of surprise was its chief characteristic."

Charles bowled his most perfect donkey drop of all at Brentwood. The victim, Gordon Barker, was well set on 44. "He tossed it right up in the air, miles up in the air," Barker remembers, "and I started by thinking I was going to hit it over mid on, then I was going to hit it over mid-wicket, then over square leg and in the end I was going to hit it over the keeper's head. And it dropped right on top of the bails. I couldn't do anything else but laugh!"

"It was just before lunch," Charles recalls. "I don't remember him being all that amused."

Such donkey drops had been bowled occasionally in the Victorian age, and Charles is a great lover of Arthur Conan Doyle's story 'Spedegue's Dropper': "It tells how a young man in some remote village strings a rope at the top of two tall trees and bowling over it to a wicket beyond, perfects this type of delivery. He then goes on to graduate through all levels of cricket to eventual success in a Test match."

In recent years, in an attempt to outlaw the fast beamer, the laws have been revised to prohibit the bowling of all high full-tosses. "But I don't know why," Charles says. "It can't be compared to a beamer, which is undoubtedly dangerous. I can only see any danger if some careless batsman, while looking upwards, impales himself on the wicket."

Charles was 38 years old in May 1957, and he decided that he would retire at the end of the summer. He had raised the team to new heights, but they had fallen back and now a fresh captain was needed to take them forward again. The club might have turned to Tony Diment, but the preoccupation with having an amateur in charge was receding and Charles spent the summer on the lookout around the other counties for a player of quality.

At Hull in early July he was having a drink after play with Yorkshire's Willie Watson, and he asked him if he knew anybody on the circuit who might be interested. There was a five-year contract on offer and Watson, now 37 and knowing that Yorkshire could dispense with his services at any time, was quick to reply. 'Yes,' he said. 'I might be interested.'

Away from his native Yorkshire, Willie Watson was an immediate success at Leicester. In each of his first two summers he came second in the national averages and he won back a place in the England team.

So, with the succession arranged, Charles was able to bow out as captain with no misgivings. Though he was past his very best, he was still one of the county's most reliable two batsmen, alongside the young Maurice Hallam, and his innings against Frank Tyson late in his final summer revealed a new dimension to his stroke play.

His batting had always been characterised by swift footwork, sweetness of timing, with strong wrists and a good range of shots, especially on the off side, but against Tyson that day in August 1957 he adopted a different approach.

Few players of that time have much doubt about Frank Tyson: he was the fastest bowler they ever faced. Lol Spence remembers encountering him in a second team match on a glass-like surface at the Wyggeston Boys School ground. "Percy Davis was in charge of Northants Seconds. He said, 'We've got the fastest bowler in England playing for us today.' Yes, he was quick!"

"No doubt about it," Tony Diment agrees. "He was very, very quick. I remember one match where the ball hit the peak of my cap as it went past. They said they could see my face change colour from the pavilion."

Jeff Goodwin reckons that the Northampton groundsman prepared his pitches so that Tyson could bowl in tandem with George Tribe, the Australian chinaman bowler. "At one end you'd got no grass at all and all pebbles and what have you, and at the other you'd got thick grass. One match we were walking off and the groundsman came up to Charles. 'Which roller do you want put on it, skipper?' And Charles said, 'Never mind the roller. Put the bloody Hoover on that end, will you?'"

But at Grace Road in August 1957 Charles decided to take on Tyson. It was his last month as captain of Leicestershire, and he was not pleased with the performances of his team. His first innings 50 had been out of a total of only 167, and at the end of the second day they were 96 for five, with a lead of only 23. Charles alone – on 44 not out – was showing any appetite for the contest.

Tony Diment was among those dismissed: bowled Tyson, 0. "I treated him with a lot of respect because I had to. I had rather a high backlift, I must admit, but I was still on my backlift when my off stump was wheeling back."

"It was a good wicket," Charles recalls, "Tyson was tamed to a certain extent by the wicket. But in the middle of the night I heard rain, and this was in the days when wickets were not covered. And I knew that where we were playing on the square was the most hideous place for the ball to start flying around if it was rain affected. So, when I went in with Firth the next morning, I thought, 'How on earth am I going to fly the flag by getting behind the line of the ball because this bloke was sending it whizzing past my left ear, then past my right ear?'"

"We were making a hash of it," Tony Diment says, "and Charles got rather irritable that we weren't doing very well. He went in and he said, 'I'll show you how to play this man.'"

Before Charles faced a ball on the final morning, George Tribe took three wickets with his first four balls, and Leicestershire were 96 for eight. "They went down like ninepins," Charles says, "and I still hadn't taken strike. So, when I did face Tyson, I'd lost this awful feeling that I'd got to bat through, so I went at it with gay abandon. I thought, 'There's only another couple of wickets left, so I can do what I like.'

Terry Spencer remembers how he set about it: "When Frank Tyson delivered, Charles took one step to leg and crashed him through the off side. Frankie was getting madder and madder, and the faster he bowled the harder Charles whacked him to the boundary."

"He took one step back and thrashed," says Tony Diment, "and they'd be going over slips' heads, they'd be going everywhere, but it had the effect of taming Tyson a bit because he'd never had treatment like this before."

"I went down the track to Tyson," Charles says. "It was a fascinating thing to do. To his eternal credit he never tried to hit me. He only tried to bowl a bouncer from a tactical point of view. So he kept it up to me, and I kept crashing it through the covers with a great long follow through. Had he decided to be nasty and follow me, it would have been a different story, but he didn't."

'The bespectacled Palmer,' wrote *Wisden*, 'although worried by misty rain, attacked scientifically, hitting 35 of the 36 runs added in half an hour.' But Terry Spencer was bowled by Tyson for a duck, the lumbering Brian Boshier was run out for one, and Leicestershire ended on 132 all out, with Charles undefeated on 79.

Three weeks later, in the final home match of the season, he hit 103 against Essex, the last of his 24 centuries for the county.

His departure was marked by the award of a testimonial and a farewell dinner. "A fair bit of wine flowed," says Tony Diment. "Charles got up and made a masterly speech, and something that has stuck in my mind is that he managed to get the phrase 'avuncular benignity' into it. He was so proud of it, he said, 'I shall say that again, avuncular benignity.' And to this day I don't know what it means!"

There was a presentation of a walnut table and an illuminated manuscript bearing the autographs of all the players. The Supporters' Club gave Charles a silver tray with a coffee set and, at the Annual Ball, Neville Dowen presented him with a canteen of cutlery on behalf of the members.

*   *   *

What had the quiet schoolmaster achieved on the field of play during his years at Leicestershire?

As a batsman he finished in the top two of the county averages in each of his eight summers and, when he finally retired, after a few holiday matches in 1958 and 1959, he had scored 12,587 runs for the county. It was an age of three-day matches on uncovered pitches, and the only Leicestershire batsman before him to finish with an average better than his 33.04 was the New Zealander CS Dempster, who had played four summers before the war.

As a bowler he took 291 wickets for the county and his average of 22.56 is lower than that of any of his contemporaries, even the Australians Vic Jackson and Jack Walsh. Further, he conceded his runs at a rate of only 1.89 an over, where even the most niggardly bowlers of the time – Derek Shackleton, Don Shepherd, Brian Statham and Les Jackson – went for more than two an over.

He did not bowl enough to be considered a fully-fledged all-rounder, but the ratio of his batting to bowling average finished at 1.46 and this stands favourable comparison with all the leading English all-rounders of the post-war period: Trevor Bailey 1.44, Ray Illingworth 1.38, Bill Edrich 1.27, Ian Botham 1.25, Tony Greig 1.08 and Fred Titmus 1.03.

Then there was his captaincy. It was not as fiercely competitive as Stuart Surridge at The Oval or Glamorgan's Wilf Wooller – "When I went out to bat against Glamorgan," tail-ender Jeff Goodwin recalls, "Wooller would bring up all the fielders. But Charles was too much of a gentleman to do that." Nor did the players feel that that his captaincy was as tactically astute as, say, Ray Illingworth, who became county captain in 1969. "Charles was a schoolmaster type," Terry Spencer says. "He tended to do things by numbers."

"A good straightforward captain," says Reg Simpson, Notts skipper at this time. "If he saw something was required, he'd do it."

"He was thoughtful but fairly orthodox," Doug Insole, the Essex captain, says. "He was always sportingly inclined. He'd go for a result if he possibly could, and he wouldn't pull back. Some captains would be 40 for three and say, 'Bugger this, we'll pack it in.' But not Charles. If he accepted a challenge, he went on to the limit."

"He was a great bloke," Insole adds. "But he was by no means a soft touch. He was quite a hard nut tactically on the field."

Those who played under Charles all agree that he was a great handler of people, a man who maintained discipline in a kindly way. "He never lost his temper," Jeff Goodwin says, "yet he'd got quite a firm way of saying how he wanted things doing. And he always looked after the players if there were any problems. He was a very good listener. Some captains didn't want that side of it. They just wanted to captain the side on the field, and that was it."

"He always seemed to have time for you," Lol Spence says. "He was a proper gentleman." And Lol's wife Hermine, who worked in the office when Charles was Chairman, says the same. "A lot of the people would just walk through the office, but he'd speak to you and ask how you were."

"You gave him respect because he was a gentleman," says Ray Julian, a youngster starting in Charles' last years. "I played under several captains at Leicester: Willie Watson, Maurice Hallam, Ray Illingworth, Tony Lock, David Kirby. And, as a leader of men, I think Charles Palmer was one of the best."

* * *

When Charles left Leicestershire County Cricket Club, he joined Richards of Leicester, a steel company owned by William Richards, the benefactor who provided leather bags for the players.

"I went there at the behest of the old man and his two sons. They took a lot of trouble over me because I was totally non-engineering, non-everything. They put me in the foundry, to familiarise me with the business."

It was another world from schoolmastering and administering cricket, and his early efforts when he rolled up his sleeves did not make much of an impression. "I was no damn good as a foundryman at all, but the other foundrymen were delightful people, right down to earth. I'd be making a complete mess of pouring metal into a mould and they'd say, 'Oh leave that, Charlie, I'll do it for you.'"

It was a great culture shock, not least having to adapt to an employer like Mr Richards. "He was in every sense the boss. It was he who had kept the company going in hard times, and he held everybody in thrall through sheer personality. He ruled with a rod of iron."

Mr Richards, with Charles

The Chairman's daily arrival was a noteworthy event. "It was about 700 or 800 yards down the road to the works gates and, as he turned down the road, he used to put his hand on the horn, so everybody in the place would be saying, 'Here's Mr Richards. Here's Mr Richards.' And he'd keep it there until he swept in through the gates.

"He'd walk into the foundry in highly polished shoes and, if he got a bit of dust on his shoes, he'd play hell. And all over the place were notices: 'No smoking ... Smoking forbidden ... Anyone caught smoking will be subject to instant dismissal.' He was the sort of person who made himself responsible for all sorts of silly things: 'I'm the person who's responsible for buying string.'"

When his period of training ended, Charles was assigned to Richards Structural Steel, a subsidiary managed by one of the old man's sons, 'Mr Philip' – or 'Dickie', as Charles learnt to call him on the golf course. "He was a really civilised guy. And, thank God, I was thrown into his lap."

Philip Richards was a sportsman of distinction. He played golf off a handicap of one, had been a Corinthian footballer and, in Charles' view, could have played county cricket as a wicket-keeper, had his father allowed it. Moreover, Charles found that he had a first-class business brain.

Soon Charles was travelling about the world, selling a new product Thorite – invented by two Leicester men – for use in mines and quarries. Before he visited Australia, he rang Ronnie Aird, MCC secretary, to check the schedule of West Indies' tour – but, alas, he was unable to adjust his itinerary. "I was there at the time they had that tied Test match at Brisbane. But I was in Perth. Nobody will believe me, and I don't blame them, but I never saw a day's cricket on the whole trip."

He remained with the company for 25 years and, despite his frequent trips abroad, he still found time to serve Leicestershire County Cricket Club.

CHAPTER 16

PRESIDENT OF MCC

"It was a Sunday morning," Charles says, thinking back to the spring of 1978. "I was reading the paper in bed when the bedside phone rang. To my surprise, it was David Clark of Kent, an old friend. We were both county captains at the same time, we'd played golf together, and we'd got to know each other very well. At the time he was President of MCC.

"He said to me, 'Will you do something for me?' I said, 'Of course, if I can.' He continued, 'I would like to nominate you as President Designate of MCC. Will you accept nomination?' So I mumbled something to the effect that I had just seen the newspaper and that it said it was April the first. And he said, 'That's irrelevant.' So I said, 'I can't think of a greater honour. I would love to do it, but may I first speak to my company chairman?'"

Amid his pride and delight, Charles admits to having had "a certain feeling of trepidation because one knew one was following people who had done the job very well, and there was self-doubt as to whether one could do as well for the good of the club."

An early priority was to clear the way for long periods of absence from his employment. Although he had only a hazy idea what the presidency might entail, Charles found his chairman keen to do all he could to make it possible. "It's a great honour," said Dickie Richards. "You won't get another chance. Keep us informed of your movements and when you will be away."

As his many friends across the cricket world wrote to share his joy and wish him well, an aerogramme from Australia, sent direct to Lord's, gave Charles especial pleasure. An old adversary from that never-to-be-forgotten day at Worcester in 1948, Keith Miller, wrote: 'Charles, I was delighted. Over the many years, I have known many Presidents, but you are the first one I have written to with congratulations.'

For Miller it brought back memories of his first ever match as a touring Australian. 'Palmer thumping our pretty useful attack around to score 80 odd – one of the best innings I saw that season. Nostalgia. I derive great pleasure thinking of things like this of the past.'

'Dear Parley Charmer', wrote Brian Sellers, the great force of Yorkshire cricket. 'When I saw David Clark at Old Trafford last year, I told him I thought that the powers that be at Lord's had really got to the bottom of the barrel. But now I know they hadn't. It's dropped out!'

Charles Palmer was a break with tradition in the MCC presidency. He was the son of a salesman, he had been to grammar school and to a redbrick university, and he had played his cricket for two Midland counties. 'It is high time,' one letter of congratulation read, 'that someone like yourself, who is not from the South nor from the old school crowd, and who has rendered such distinguished service to the game, was recognised.'

Cricket was in a period of global difficulty, and it was clear that there were challenges ahead for the President. 'What a mess cricket is in at the moment,' wrote Sellers in wishing Charles 'every success and God knows that you will need it when you take office.' Miller, meanwhile, expressed similar sentiments: 'I'm afraid I find it hard to get enthusiastic these days. May be old age. May be the advent of Packer.'

Kerry Packer was the Australian media mogul whose World Series Cricket was the first dark cloud to hang over Charles' year of office. As MCC President, Charles was also Chairman of the International Cricket Conference, whose member countries were struggling to cope with Packer's aggressive intervention. Enraged by the refusal of the Australian cricket authorities to grant him television rights to their Tests, Packer had set about signing up many of the world's best players for his own matches. His methods were clandestine, and in English cricket circles nothing had made him more unpopular than the discovery that he had secretly enlisted the reigning England captain, Tony Greig, as one of his chief recruiting agents.

When ICC had attempted to retaliate by barring players from Test and county cricket, Packer sued. Moral indignation rather the legal merits of their case persuaded ICC to defend their actions in the High Court in London, where they suffered a comprehensive and humiliating defeat. "Mr Justice Slade found against us," Charles remembers, "probably quite rightly, and it cost us £250,000, a lot of money in those days."

While the presidency meant that Charles could enjoy a pleasant trip to Australia to watch England retain the Ashes against a second-string Australian side, he was soon required to return with his predecessor David Clark and with Jack Bailey, Secretary of MCC and the ICC. Their mission was to meet with Packer and to find some way back from the chaos into which international cricket had been thrown.

Buoyed up by his success in court, Packer's World Series matches were going ahead for a second year. Using ingeniously prepared drop-in pitches, they were staged on fairgrounds, trotting parks and other unlikely venues through the Australian summer. "It was his way," Charles thinks, "of saying 'Bugger you. If you won't let me play on your grounds, I'll build my own.' That is what he did, and very successfully in a way."

With coloured clothing and day-night matches, the games did not lack innovation and razzmatazz. Yet crowds never flocked to the grounds in the numbers that Packer and his organisation had hoped.

The conflict between Packer and the cricket authorities had been the dominant business in the year before Charles took office. "I was tail-end Charlie, picking it up after Tagge Webster and David Clark. My brief was to keep the dialogue with Packer going and to see what we could do to get rid of him and to maintain the traditional game.

"But how the hell did I approach the man? He was a different animal from me. I remember rehearsing what I was going to say to the chap. In fact I wrote a phantom letter, putting it all on a jovial footing: 'Look, apparently we're going to meet, but it looks as though we don't see eye to eye on a number of points. And I know you could eat six of me for breakfast. I just hope you won't throw me into the Tasman Sea.'"

Charles recalls that the temperature was over 100° as he made his way to Packer's Sydney office with Clark and Bailey. "I'd got to the stage of thinking, 'I haven't got very much to lose. He can toss me into the Tasman Sea if he wishes, but whether that will get him anywhere I don't know.' He didn't want to talk to me because he was riding high. He was on a roll; he had got all the players that he wanted.

"And the Australians also didn't want me to talk to Packer because they thought that I might give away some of their preserve. So I had to go and talk to someone who didn't want to speak to me on behalf of someone who didn't want me to speak to him!"

"The Australian hierarchy were a little bit double standards about it," Jack Bailey says. "They sought us out at a time when Packer was threatening to take away their game. Then, when it had gone on for a year or two, they started talking to Packer and were rather resentful of anyone else being involved at all. So it was rather like a drowning man waving an arm and you get him out of the sea, then go and visit him afterwards and he says, 'What the hell are you doing here?'"

The great rapprochement was round the corner. Packer had come to realise that his matches would never be the equal of official Tests, while the Board, yearning for the return of a successful national team, could appreciate that there were benefits beyond mere money in granting Packer the television rights he sought and, as events would prove, allowing him to dictate aspects of the international schedule.

But none of this was known to Charles as he and his party were greeted by Packer.

"I remember old Packer. It was 'D'ya wanna drink?' in about that tone. I said, 'Yes, I'm thirsty.' He gave me something – I don't know what it was – and I must have registered something less than delight at what I was drinking, because he said, 'Don't you like that?' I said, 'It's all right.' Then he said to one of his minions, 'Get him another one. Get him a gin and tonic, or something.' I said, 'You can't afford to throw drinks away.'"

The burly, aggressively self-seeking Kerry Packer, one of the richest men in Australia, and the diminutive, self-effacing and whimsical Charles Palmer: how ill-matched they must have seemed! And how little common ground they shared. "I didn't like him," says Charles. "He was a bombast, and I didn't like what he was doing. I didn't like his approach. But then he probably didn't like me either." In Jack Bailey's eyes, Packer changed the mindset of cricket. "It wasn't a game any longer, it was a business. It wasn't so much making money in order to play cricket, it was playing cricket in order to make money."

Charles recalls little of the meeting beyond the opening exchange. "It was,

'What do you want to talk to me about?' 'Well, since you ask me, how best to get rid of you.' It wasn't exactly a happy meeting."

In the wake of Packer, money began to flow into cricket. Sponsors paid more for their privileges, and the top players were better rewarded. The one-day game eventually embraced the added theatre of coloured clothing and day-night matches that Packer had pioneered. "It was all anathema to the traditionalist," Charles says. "In those days we were all very old-fashioned. We had been entrenched in our way of playing cricket for God knows how many decades. In retrospect, I think quite a number of decent things came of it all. Taking a long-term view, some of the things were good for some of the players, but whether they were good for cricket it's difficult to say."

There was only a brief respite before he was flying off once more on another challenging and fraught trip, this time to South Africa, a country whose players had been denied Test cricket for the best part of a decade. The President of the recently formed non-racial South African Cricket Union, Rashid Varachia, had written to Charles. "He asked if I would take a delegation of ICC people over there to investigate for ourselves the degree to which they had tried to get rid of apartheid in South African cricket."

The mission was doomed before they set off. "I failed to get a representative party. The Indians wouldn't come, the West Indians wouldn't come, nor would the Pakistanis. No coloured people would come except, of all people, a chap from Bermuda." Bermuda was by this time an associate member of the ICC, and their representative, Alma Hunt, found himself alongside exclusively white delegates from Australia, New Zealand and the United States, the latter a gentleman whom Charles recalls as "a very rich man with nothing to do."

Bob Parrish (Australia), Alma Hunt (Bermuda), Murray Chapple (New Zealand),
Charles Palmer (England), Walter Hadlee (New Zealand), John Gardiner (USA),
Boon Wallace (South African Cricket Union)

Still with a soft spot for the country whose hospitality he had enjoyed as a touring cricketer, Charles now found himself full of admiration for those who were doing their best, in the face of the unyielding rule of apartheid, to bring black and white players together on the cricket field. "Joe Pamensky was the hard worker. Varachia was slightly more of a figurehead, but enormously respected. And Boon Wallace, he was a wonderful man, I thought. He worked extremely hard and got hit on the head so many times by all sorts of people."

The delegates travelled to Johannesburg and Cape Town, and they visited the township of Soweto. "We saw the poorer sides of Soweto, but also one or two nice houses and some nice cars. There was a chap there doing a wonderful job coaching the young Africans. I was very sad that we couldn't do anything to help them. But that was the way of the world."

Looking back, Charles recalls the trip as "interesting but fruitless. All the officials, the whites, were trying very hard to get rid of apartheid in the game, but it was a dead duck to try to get integration. Apartheid was apartheid.

"I knew in my heart of hearts that it was only a morale booster for them, an effort to give them some feeling that they were not isolated, that we had not forgotten them. It was not practical for them to return to international cricket and, when we got back home and took it to the annual meeting of the ICC at Lord's, they laughed us out of court."

Charles was accompanied by the Secretary of MCC. "He was a clever chap, Jack Bailey. I had a great respect for his brain. And he wrote a very good report, I thought, on what SACU had managed to achieve."

President and Secretary: Charles Palmer and Jack Bailey

But the merits of the report were not even debated at Lord's. Delegates from Pakistan, India and West Indies were incensed that a delegation they had refused to join should have suggested that it was representing ICC. Moreover, with the Gleneagles Agreement now discouraging sporting contacts with South Africa, they opposed any examination of the state of cricket in South Africa. To the disappointment of Charles, they insisted that Bailey's report should not be discussed. The press statement agreed at the meeting was therefore worded to describe Charles, Jack Bailey and the others as travelling 'in their individual capacities', though it did allow a commendation of 'the progress made by the SACU to establish non-racial and normal cricket in South Africa.'

Some delegates from South Africa had travelled to London in the hope of being able to address the full ICC meeting. "I said, 'Can we bring the South Africans in to plead their case?' Well some people said, 'Yes'. They were obviously the entrenched people on one side, but there were equally entrenched people on the other. Then I think it was Australia who said, 'Why don't we, instead of allowing them to come in, adjourn the meeting and ask them to come and talk to us during the adjournment?' So the South Africans were permitted to meet people in an adjourned meeting. It wobbled about a bit, but they were satisfied that they had had a chance to talk to people."

Charles' time as President of MCC was not all hard politics, though. A highlight of every President's term is the Lord's Test, when his box is filled each day with fellow officers in the world of cricket, representatives of sponsoring companies and personal friends. Charles' year in office was marked by another very special occasion at Lord's, the final of the second World Cup, with Mike Brearley's England team reaching the final. The day ended in brilliant sunshine, with a West Indian victory.

Less satisfying was the Test match against India, where rain claimed almost nine hours of playing time, though Charles still retains a file of letters of thanks from those who enjoyed his hospitality.

One of the distinguished guests in his box was Sir George Edwards, former Chairman of British Aircraft Corporation, now President of Surrey County Cricket Club. Barbara, with an interest in aircraft that dated back to her wartime service as a radar operator tracking the movement of planes and flying bombs, got into conversation with him. "She asked him, 'What makes an aeroplane fly?' Well, rather than scoffing or anything like that, he brought a well-sharpened pencil out of his jacket and drew squiggles all over the luncheon table.

"Barbara also told him a story of when she was plotting aircraft in the Coventry area. She was plotting a very strong signal, which was travelling, according to the data, at something like 500 miles an hour. Her officer said, 'You silly idiot. How can you be plotting something at 500 miles an hour? Tempest is only just over 300.' George Edwards questioned her and he said, 'Do you know what I think? I don't think you were being stupid at all. I think it was one of Frank Whittle's experimental jet planes, which flew from Lutterworth nearby.' He said, 'I bet you'd like to see your officer now and have a word with him after our conversation!'"

Dennis Silk, later to become MCC President himself, recalls the fun that characterised a box hosted by the Palmers. "They both did a wonderful job,

Charles and his dear wife. I first got to know Charles when I was playing with Somerset, and I took to him immediately for his wonderful sense of humour, his ability to mock himself. I can't think of anyone who was more popular in the ranks of first-class cricketers.

"He was an extremely impressive Chairman of TCCB. Everybody admired the job he did. He could be serious when he needed to be serious, and he could be light-hearted when that was appropriate. I simply have never heard a word against Charles. He was very good at quietly putting people down in a gentle way and sorting things out before they became matters of state. A man you would find it very difficult to quarrel with. He could always see the other man's point of view, and there are not many around who can do that.

"He was always extremely well prepared for meetings. It must have been his time as a schoolmaster that got him into that habit. He took meetings extremely crisply and was always prepared to say when he hadn't got an immediate answer. And he always knew who to turn to give the right answer.

"It's worth saying that whenever a serious issue came up, he could be very strong indeed. Not someone to be dismissed lightly. People listened to him, partly because they liked him and partly because he had a first-class mind, a very clear mind. Amidst all the fun and friendliness, when a matter of high principle came along, he was real steel."

Charles deflects the praise in the direction of the MCC Secretary: "Jack Bailey was immaculate in the way he ran things. The presentation of the agenda was always a masterpiece. Jack thought of every question that could be asked, and your answer as president was what he had put down. He was very good."

Tradition dies hard at Lord's, and Charles was touched that he should receive, in the year of his presidency, a membership pass bearing the number 'one'. He was honoured, too, that it should fall to him to be at Buckingham Palace to introduce to Her Majesty the Queen the 22 teams that came to compete in the Prudential World Cup and the ICC Associate Members World Cup Competition that preceded it.

He also attended the final of the Cricketer Cup, the competition for old boys of the public schools. The match at Burton Court in Chelsea was won by Tonbridge, whose prize was a trip to Epernay to visit the headquarters of Moet and Chandon, the French sponsor. Charles was invited to accompany them.

They were flown out in a private bi-plane and at Epernay they were wined and dined, after which their host treated them to one of his special party tricks – opening a bottle of champagne with a ceremonial sword. They all watched as the Frenchman waved the sword above his head and then brought it down on the bottle. "He did it in front of all of us," says Charles, "and he missed.

"I remember when we came back on the plane. The stewardess came up and said, 'Would you like a glass of champagne?' I said, 'No thank you. Can I have a glass of water?'"

There were other overseas trips: a goodwill mission, accompanied by

Barbara, to Fiji and New Zealand, and a return to India where he marvelled at the changes to the Eden Gardens ground in Calcutta where he had played during the war. "In those days it had had a capacity of 10,000. Now it held 100,000 people, all choc a bloc, with 100,000 outside waiting to come in."

It involved more time away from his work in Leicester than Charles had anticipated, and he recalls how, when he did return one day, the chairman greeted him with a wry look. "Can we re-appraise our arrangements?" Dickie Richards suggested. "Don't tell me when you are going to be away; tell me when you will be here."

"He was a very co-operative man to work for," Charles says. "In fact, for my time with MCC that year, I was in effect being given a sabbatical."

It was a hard-working sabbatical, but on MCC business he travelled in style. "I always remember – it amused me and it still does – they booked me first class to go to Australia. A hell of a price. I said, 'You needn't have done that.' They said, 'You are President of the biggest club in the world; you should go up in the front.' We landed in Pakistan, and I was sitting in the front in first class and I thought, 'Thank God I am'. Because cars with flags flying came up to this plane, and all I had to do was walk down the steps. Just imagine the ignominy of all of them waiting if I had had to walk all the way to the back of the aeroplane."

Charles looks back on the year as the high peak of his service to cricket. It was an honour and a privilege far beyond anything he might have imagined when he had taken the bold decision to abandon the comfortable life of teaching at a public school in favour of a position as captain and secretary of an almost bankrupt county cricket club. Back then, in the early months of 1950, the MCC President had been none other than His Royal Highness The Duke of Edinburgh, shortly to be succeeded by Sir Pelham Warner. They inhabited a distant peak far beyond the aspirations of a young man with a background like that of Charles.

"There were two great watersheds in my life. The first was when the Australians came in 1948 and I managed to get some runs. The second was when I became President of MCC. It widened my horizons, not only in cricket but in life. Meeting everybody and travelling the world. And travelling the world, I'm happy to say – it wouldn't happen today, perhaps – with a red carpet laid out."

CHAPTER 17

TOWARDS RETIREMENT

The MCC presidency passed from Charles to his chosen successor Billy Griffith, but his work at Lord's was far from over. Immediately he was installed as Chairman of the Cricket Council, the umbrella body under which the Test and County Cricket Board, the National Cricket Association and MCC had an equal voice in the governance of the national game. "It was fun," he says, "but what was my function on the Cricket Council? It had got no teeth."

Four years later, he was elected to the more influential role of Chairman of the TCCB. "It was a very time-consuming job. It was much more hands on than the presidency of MCC, and much more commercial of course. I'd got to the stage where I was nearing retirement when I took that on. We had a flat in London at that time; it was that hands on."

The power of MCC had been reduced in 1968 when public funding for cricket became available and could not be granted to a private members' club. Thus the Cricket Council was created, and – with its constitution revised and reviewed repeatedly – there was much confusion at Lord's. "When MCC was God in the cricket world," Charles says, "everything was always MCC's fault. Then it ceased to have the impact that it had had before, and people didn't know who the hell they were talking about and who they were talking to and who was responsible for what. It takes time for these sorts of things to evolve."

Many of those serving on committees moved freely between MCC and TCCB. Some, like Charles himself, Doug Insole and George Mann, sat on both bodies at the same time. Inevitably disputes arose, and those wearing two hats could easily find their loyalties divided or compromised.

In 1982, in Charles' fourth year as Chairman of the Cricket Council, a working party proposed radical changes to the administrative structure of cricket in Britain. Weaknesses in the processes of decision-making had been exposed during the Kerry Packer court case, and the three-man working party, under the chairmanship of Raman Subba Row, proposed – among other things – that a new governing body be created, with MCC's representation cut from five to one.

Though the full proposal was not adopted, the membership of the Cricket Council was altered to reflect the growing power of those who ran the professional game. Where the three constituent parties had previously held five seats each, now the Test and County Cricket Board were awarded eight, the National Cricket Association (representing the recreational game) kept five and MCC was reduced to only three.

'Gubby' Allen, the former England captain and still the most influential figure at Lord's, wrote to Charles, expressing his deep resentment at MCC's loss of voice and tendering his resignation from the Council. A veteran of the Bodyline tour, he was now in his eighties, but in the musical chairs that ensued he soon reappeared at Council meetings, this time as a representative of the TCCB!

Lord's Cricket Ground became a source of friction between MCC and TCCB. "The Board were aiming to get greater use of Lord's," Charles explains. "And Jack Bailey didn't like that. 'I'm going to protect my members.' He fought very hard for that. It was mostly about the use of facilities: boxes for sponsors and if someone wanted to bring fifty people in as guests and so on. Jack and David Clark would say, 'This is MCC's prerogative, to do what they think is right. It's their ground, it's their club.' And the people on the other side would say, 'Well we've got to look after everybody.' But you can't look after everybody at Lord's. There isn't room, there isn't time. And so we had that dichotomy of interests. There was a possibility of Jack's empire being eroded, and he didn't want that."

"Nor did I want it," Charles adds, betraying his instinctive allegiance to the cause of MCC despite now wearing a TCCB hat. His talent for keeping the peace was clearly tested and, when he passed the Chairmanship of the TCCB and the Cricket Council to Raman Subba Row, the TCCB cause gained unstoppable momentum. By the end of the next year Jack Bailey had resigned as Secretary of MCC.

In the wider world, Charles discovered, it was still the name of MCC that carried most sway. In February 1980, as Chairman of the Cricket Council, he attended the Golden Jubilee celebrations of the Indian Board of Control. "I had this grandiloquent title," he says. "But I was still talked about as the President of MCC. Nobody over there knew the difference between the Cricket Council, the TCCB or Uncle Tom Cobley."

England sent a team to play a single Test at the Wankhede Stadium in Bombay, a match dominated by Ian Botham with a century and eleven wickets, and the hosts threw a massive party at the Taj Mahal, the city's leading hotel and one of the finest in the world at that time. "It was like a big wedding," says Charles. "Michael Melford wrote a lovely piece about it in the *Daily Telegraph* to say that this was a very auspicious occasion, which the Indians organised extremely well. Five hundred people were invited, 800 turned up and three people listened to the speeches."

His chairmanship of the Cricket Council made Charles one of the United Kingdom's representatives on the ICC. So he still maintained contact with old friends in South African cricket, and he made a further trip there to help publicise the progress the game's administrators were making towards integration. Charles and Barbara were invited to Johannesburg as a special guests at a large 'Sporting Greats' banquet.

"They wanted a name, and the biggest name they could find in cricket was the Chairman of the English Cricket Council. I thought, 'What have I got to lose?' It was a well publicised, televised dinner, which I thought they did extremely well, and Palmer was turned on as the Ronnie Corbett of the evening – which I quite enjoyed doing."

Once again Charles knew that he could make no promises. "It was just to say that there are many people in the world who are sympathetic to your cause but, politics being what it is, we haven't the power to implement some of those thoughts."

With his retirement from the chairmanship of the TCCB, Charles' involvement with the administration of cricket began to wind down, but his special skills as a chairman were still in demand at the TCCB. A Palmer Committee was set up, to enquire into the standards of play in cricket in the UK, with a special brief 'to maximise the good effects of limited-overs cricket and to minimise the bad ones.'

"What one had to guard against," Charles says, "was that the pendulum did not swing too far. In my view the emphasis on one-day matches had gone too far because the very essence of cricket is bowling sides out. Yet it is possible to win one-day matches simply by containing."

The committee, including Peter May, Tom Cartwright, Keith Andrew and Alan Smith, met through 1985 and in December Charles presented its findings, notably recommending changes to the structure of the County Championship. These were summarised by the magazine *The Cricketer*, as follows:

Sixteen three-day and eight four-day matches, the latter to be played over weekends, including Sunday play. All Championship games to be played on pitches which would be uncovered during the hours of play (except for bowler's run-up and follow-through areas). Bonus points to be awarded for bowling only. Increased prize money for the Championship and higher compensation for counties who provide England players.

Inevitably many of the report's recommendations were consigned to the very 'waste-paper basket' that Charles hoped that they would avoid when he introduced the report at a press conference, but at least their radical proposal for four-day cricket was introduced in 1988, becoming the norm for all county matches in 1993.

On 31st March 1989 Charles' 25-year reign as Chairman of Leicestershire came to an end. "If I would like people to remember me in any way," he said when he stepped down, "it would be as someone who has put back something into a game which gave him great pleasure."

While he was still Chairman, the county had already turned to Charles when the presidency became vacant. First taking office in 1987, he was persuaded to extend his term, finally retiring in 1993. Roger Goadby, Treasurer of the county at the time and a later Chairman, remembers Charles' term of office: "He didn't say a lot but, when he did, you listened and learned from it. He dealt with everything in a calm and dignified way and everybody listened intently while he was speaking."

Even after stepping down as President, Charles remained a familiar figure at the county's matches, retaining a keen interest in affairs and making a point of attending former players' reunions. His service to the game was marked by the award of the CBE in 1984. Then in 1991 he was elected an Honorary Life Vice-President of MCC, joining a small band of only seven others, headed by Sir Donald Bradman. At Grace Road in 1996, the Members' Room and Pavilion Restaurant was formally reopened as the Charles Palmer Suite – in honour of the man who, among so many achievements at Leicester, had introduced the football pool that had made such facilities possible.

Barbara and Charles: first guests in the new Charles Palmer Suite

Withdrawing from the day-to-day concerns of the county club gave Charles more time for family and leisure. Elder son Andrew, a ship's engineer, and Tim, now back in England after 25 years abroad, both speak of their father with obvious affection and pride, making special mention of his wit and talent for self-deprecation. "The gentlemanliness and the sense of humour, that's probably the most enduring thing I'm proud of with him," says Tim, "It's very difficult to imagine anyone not enjoying his company."

When Charles and Barbara visited Tim and his family in Canada in 1996, Leicestershire were on the verge of winning their second Championship title, 21 years after Ray Illingworth's 1975 triumph. Desperate to keep in touch with their progress in the final round of matches, Charles set up an elaborate system of phone calls to keep him abreast of the score. "But it was all usurped by my teenage daughter," says Tim. "She went onto the internet and brought through a complete score and online report as it happened and gave it to my father. He thought it was complete magic. She thought it was quite normal, though she hadn't a clue what she was handing him. He was absolutely mesmerised by modern science."

Despite attending a computer course, Charles always remained happier with pen and paper. The arts held more attraction than the sciences. Though his fingers grew less supple at the piano, he and Barbara continued to enjoy local concerts. He also signed up for art classes, where he revealed a considerable latent skill as a painter.

There was a year as captain of the Leicestershire Golf Club that lies close to the home where Charles and Barbara have lived for over fifty years. Still playing when well into his eighties, Charles is no more inclined to boast of his golfing achievements than he is of those on the cricket field:

"I was in a four-ball 'friendly' match at the club, and I was being bombarded by this chap, who kept asking me asinine questions on cricket. 'Did I do this? ... Did I do that? ... Did you ever go to Australia?' I said, 'Yes, I did.' 'And did you ever score a century there?' 'Yes,' I said. 'As a matter of fact, I did.' 'Oh, where was that?' 'At the Royal Sydney Golf Club,' I said, with undisguised glee. End of bombardment!"

REMARKABLE BOWLING ANALYSES

TEN WICKETS IN AN INNINGS

19.4	16	10	10	H. Verity (Yorks)	v Notts, Leeds	1932
16.2	8	18	10	G. Geary (Leics)	v Glamorgan, Pontypridd	1929
19	11	20	10	P.M. Chatterjee (Bengal)	v Assam, Jorhat	1956-57
12	2	26	10	A.E. Vogler (E. Province)	v Griqualand W, Johannesburg	1906-07

NINE WICKETS IN AN INNINGS

19	17	2	9	G. Elliott (Victoria)	v Tasmania, Launceston	1857-58
6.3	4	7	9	Ahad Khan (Railways)	v Dera Ismail Khan, Lahore	1964-65
10	4	11	9	A.P. Freeman (Kent)	v Sussex, Brighton	1922
6.3	3	12	9	H. Verity (Yorks)	v Kent, Sheffield	1936

EIGHT WICKETS IN AN INNINGS

14	12	2	8	J.C. Laker (England)	v The Rest, Bradford	1950
11.1	7	4	8	D. Shackleton (Hampshire)	v Somerset, Weston-s-Mare	1955
16	11	5	8	E. Peate (Yorks)	v Surrey, Holbeck	1883
14	?	7	8	J. Bickley (England)	v Kent & Sussex, Lord's	1856
9.4	5	7	8	G.A. Lohmann (England)	v South Africa, Port Elizabeth	1895-96
14	12	7	8	C.H. Palmer (Leics)	v Surrey, Leicester	1955

SEVEN WICKETS IN AN INNINGS

8.3	6	3	7	F.R. Spofforth (Australians)	v England XI, Birmingham	1884
9.3	7	4	7	W. Henderson (NE Transvaal)	v Orange Free State, Bloemfontein	1937-38
7	4	4	7	R. Goel (Haryana)	v Jammu & Kashmir, Chandigarh	1977-78
7	5	4	7	N.W. Bracken (NSW)	v South Australia, Sydney	2004-05

SIX WICKETS IN AN INNINGS

21.2	20	1	6	S. Costick (Victoria)	v Tasmania, Melbourne	1868-69
4.5	3	1	6	V.I. Smith (South Africans)	v Derbyshire, Derby	1947
11	10	1	6	Israr Ali (Bahawalpur)	v Dacca University, Bahawalpur	1957-58
8.4	7	2	6	E.F. Field (Warwicks)	v Worcs, Dudley	1914
4.5	4	2	6	Shahid Anwar (Nat Bank)	v Pakistan Customs, Karachi	1996-97

FIVE WICKETS IN AN INNINGS

3	3	0	5	A.D. Pougher (MCC)	v Australians, Lord's	1896
6	6	0	5	G.R. Cox (Sussex)	v Somerset, Weston-s-Mare	1921
5	5	0	5	R.K. Tyldesley (Lancs)	v Leics, Manchester	1924
6.4	6	0	5	P.T. Mills (Glos)	v Somerset, Bristol	1928

Had Charles Palmer stopped bowling after his 11th or 12th over, or had Terry Spencer taken the final wicket in his 9th or 10th over, Charles would have finished with figures of 8 wickets for no runs, three more wickets than any other bowler has taken without conceding a run.

A dedicated statistician might care to pursue this, but it does seem likely that Charles' achievement in taking **eight consecutive wickets without conceding a run** is unique in first-class cricket.

A BRIEF STATISTICAL DIGEST

Charles Palmer C.B.E.

Born: 15 May 1919
Died: 31 March 2005

BATTING IN ALL FIRST-CLASS CRICKET

Year	Matches	Innings	Not Outs	Runs	Highest	Average
1938	10	15	1	205	56	14.64
1939	21	36	3	993	132	30.09
1945	1	2	0	87	77	43.50
1945/6 India	*1*	*2*	*0*	*33*	*21*	*16.50*
1946	8	14	1	252	52*	19.38
1947	8	15	1	616	177	44.00
1948	12	22	0	545	89	24.77
1948/9 South Africa	*11*	*18*	*4*	*478*	*116*	*34.14*
1949	11	19	1	722	136	40.11
1950	32	62	5	1980	143	34.73
1951	26	46	4	1699	146	40.45
1952	33	56	4	2071	127	39.82
1953	30	54	3	1645	201	32.25
1953/4 West Indies	*3*	*4*	*0*	*142*	*87*	*35.50*
1954	26	43	1	1247	107	29.69
1955	33	59	1	1857	154	32.01
1956	30	46	4	1110	120	26.42
1957	32	60	4	1436	117	25.64
1958	4	7	0	159	42	22.71
1959	4	8	1	181	53	25.85
TOTAL	**336**	**588**	**38**	**17458**	**201**	**31.74**

BATTING IN TEST CRICKET

Year	Matches	Innings	Not Outs	Runs	Highest	Average
1953/4	1	2	0	22	22	11.00

He hit 33 centuries and 98 fifties.

His highest innings were:

201	Leicestershire v Northamptonshire	Northampton	1953
177	Worcestershire v Nottinghamshire	Dudley	1947
154	Gentlemen v Players	Lord's	1955

BOWLING IN ALL FIRST-CLASS CRICKET

Year	Overs	Maidens	Runs	Wickets	Average
1938	36.5	8	103	2	51.50
1939	19	1	93	1	93.00
1945	3	0	23	0	-
1946	6	1	33	0	-
1947	144.4	32	454	14	32.42
1948	255	76	631	16	39.43
1948/9 South Africa	*30*	*7*	*64*	*5*	*12.80*
1949	265	77	698	18	38.77
1950	460.2	153	995	41	24.26
1951	384	123	819	25	32.76
1952	512.2	219	951	40	23.77
1953	390.4	177	668	31	21.54
1953/4 West Indies	*22*	*13*	*33*	*0*	*-*
1954	298.2	125	554	17	32.58
1955	447.1	187	914	48	19.04
1956	519.1	243	880	51	17.25
1957	441	180	933	42	22.21
1958	95.5	45	154	7	22.00
1959	94.1	29	183	7	26.14
TOTAL	**4424.3 †**	**1696**	**9183**	**365**	**25.15**

† includes 19 eight-ball overs in 1939
and 30 eight-ball overs in South Africa

BOWLING IN TEST CRICKET

Year	Overs	Maidens	Runs	Wickets	Average
1953/4	5	1	15	0	-

He took five wickets in an innings on five occasions.
His best figures were 14 – 12 – 7 – 8 for Leicestershire v Surrey at Leicester 1955.

He also held 147 catches.

MATCH BETWEEN LEICESTERSHIRE COUNTY CRICKET CLUB and SURREY C.C.C.

PLAYED AT LEICESTER ON May 21/23/54 19__

SIDE WINNING TOSS LEICESTERSHIRE

UMPIRES J.S. Buller and J.J. Hills

SCORERS H. Standard and H. Blossom

1st INNINGS of Innings

ORDER	Time for 50 100 / 150 200	Time IN	Time OUT	BATSMEN	RUNS AS SCORED	HOW OUT	BOWLER	Totals
1 A		3:23	3:36	CLARKE. T.H	3·3·1·	Bowled	Spencer	7
2 B		3:23	4:09	FLETCHER. D	1·2·1·2·1·	Bowled	Palmer	7
3 C		3:38	4:32	P.B.H. MAY	2·4·1·2·3·2·1·4·4·4·4·	Bowled	Palmer	28
4 D		4:34	4:40	CONSTABLE. B	/	c. Leslie	Palmer	0
5 E		4:42	4:44	STEWART. M.J	/	Bowled	Palmer	0
6 H		4:45	5:5	PRATT. R	2·4·1·	Bowled	Palmer	7
7 L		5:1	5:16	McINTYRE. A.J	/	Bowled	Palmer	0
8 M		5:7	6:0	LAKER . J.C	4·1·1·2·2·3·	Bowled	Spencer	14
9 R		5:18	5:20	SURRIDGE· W.S	/	Bowled	Palmer	0
10 S		5:22	5:37	LOCK . G.A.R	1·3·	Bowled	Palmer	4
11 T		5:39	5:40	BEDSER. A.N	2·	NOT OUT	OUT	2

BYES

LEG BYES 2. 2·2·1. ·1

WIDES

NO BALLS. ·1

TOTAL **77**

		1	2	3	4	5	6	7	8	9	10	TOTAL
FALL OF WICKETS		10	42	42	42	55	56	61	61	62	77	77
BATSMAN OUT		Clarke	May	Constable	Stewart	Kelcher	Pratt	McIntyre	Surridge	Lock	Laker	
NOT OUT		Kelcher	Kelcher	Kelcher	Kelcher	Pratt	Melaliga	Laker	Laker	Laker	Bedser	

REMARKS 50 in 72 mins. Innings lasted 137 mins.

Brilliant bowling by C.H. Palmer who took 8 wickets for 7 runs, these from 12 consecutive overs. McIntyreP took 2 wickets & took 8 wickets altogether.

The Straudwick Score Book. Copyright by H. Straudwick, Surrey County Cricket Club.

Printed by Wightman & Co., Ltd., 179, Tottenham Court Road, W.1.   Ref. 33854.

BOWLING ANALYSIS

BOWLER	Overs	Maidens	Runs	Wickets	Wides	No Balls
SPENCER. C. T	11.2	3	19	2		1
BOSHIER. B.	4	1	13	1		
MUNDEN. V.S	4	1	15	1		
JACKSON. V.E	4	3	1	1		
C.H. PALMER	14	12	7	8		
WALSH. J.E	7 4.2	3	14	1		
TOTAL	44.2		14 / 69 / 7 / 77			

Byes
Leg Byes
No Ball

THE BARCLAYS
WORLD OF CRICKET

New Edition 1980

EDITED BY E. W. SWANTON

Goodenough House 33 Old Broad Street (7th floor) London EC2P 2EE

01-283 8989

Please reply to

at Coralita
St. James
Barbados

9 February 79

Dear Charlie,

Your wire brought me up sharp, and as I sit down to
type this I blush for my effrontery. My letter was prompted by the
thought that you just might be wondering whether the time had come
to go outside the ranks of those within the close cricket circle
if anyone could be found of sufficient distinction and ability able
to give sufficient time for the job. The fact is that when the Presidency has gone beyond those concerned with cricket's admin. they've
generally been extremely good - Harold Caccia for instance, and
before him Tim Nugent. Yet I know the job is now more time-consuming
than it ever was - which enormously, I suppose, limits the choice.

The very best man of the Caccia sort in my view would be my lord
Carrington - a v. keen follower and sort of life President of High
Wycombe CC. He was a highly successful High Commissioner of Australia
and still has strong Aussie connexions (banking, I think). But if
the Tories win the election he would be hoping for the Foreign Office,
and it'd be March at the earliest before you'd know about that.
At least his advice might be of value on this assumption that an
"outside man" was a possibility.

Another political figure, Peter now Lord Rawlinson, with whom I used
to play quite a bit of club cricket, might hope to be Lord Chancellor
- though so would Hailsham for sure. Going down the scale a bit
there's Ian Orr-Ewing, a life peer, successful business man and
politician - 20-odd years MP for Hendon, 4 or five years Civil Lord
of the Admiralty, now Defence expert in the Lord's Aged 67 - still
plays for Lords and Commons ! Chairman of Harrow Wanderers. A bit
too opinionated perhaps for GOA - who might prefer Sir John Hogg,
president of Eton Ramblers, a fellow-director of the Pru and with
Caccia and distinguished merchant banker, I <u>think</u>. Sorry, no
reference books here. Aged 67 about. *

The law? I suppose one would have to look for a judge or QC who
had either retired early or kept his wits sharp into the early
seventies. Judge King-Hamilton is a good friend to MCC and speaks
well. There may well be a fruitful field here, though probably with
restricted availability - eg Sir Hugh Griffiths, Cambridge bowler
1946-8, now Recorder of somewhere, perhaps London. Carl Aarvold was
LTA boss when on the bench, I think, but demands were no doubt less.

Assistant Editors; John Woodcock, A. S. R. Winlaw, Hon W. G. Plumptre   Statistician: G. A. Copinger

Executive Editor: Hugh Montgomery-Massingberd   Produced by The Compton Press Ltd

** Later - looked him up in International who's Who at Sandy Lane.
- worked his way up to the Chairmanship of Glyn Mills. Hobbies
show cricket first.*

Getting among the Blues there's Peter Studd, ex-Lord Mayor of London, who has been mentioned before, I believe, but was then rather sick. He may now be fit - age 62. (I have my Wisden !)

I've skimmed through the blues and come on Alan Barber, retired headmaster, ex-Yorkshire captain, a marvellous chap but 74.... The name that sticks in the mind, for me, is Dennis Silk - but I won't need to sing his praises to you, I'm sure. Whether he has Radley sufficiently under control to take on the job I wouldn't know.

Such, Charlie, for what they may be worth are my thoughts which I know will be completely safe with you. I should hate it to be known that EWS had stuck his oar in uninvited since there are those who no doubt feel that strongly already. It's just that at this moment in cricket history one feels that strength and breadth at the top are so very vital.

May the good Lord be with you in these next six months - I hope you're able to keep that highly admirable "cool", come what may. I notice you said "quickly" in your wire and beg to state that this letter is finished two hours after my receiving it, and it hopes to catch the last post before the week-end this Friday afternoon. So with luck it will be at Lord's on Monday. Unhappily I foolishly omitted to bring your Leicester address here.

Yours aw

Jim

This letter was received by Charles Palmer during his year as MCC President.

He had asked EW Swanton for advice on whom he should nominate as his successor.

Knowing Swanton's own ambitions, he was perhaps being a little mischievous.

In the event he ignored Swanton's views and opted to nominate another cricket administrator, the former MCC Secretary Billy Griffith.

ACKNOWLEDGEMENTS

It has been a privilege and pleasure to write about the long life of Charles Palmer. My task has been made the easier for the time and help so freely given by his many friends in the cricket world.

I have sat and talked with: Jack Bailey, Alex Bannister, Tony Diment, Freddie Foulds, Jeff Goodwin, Guy Jarrett, John Josephs, Vic Munden, Reg Simpson, Mike Smith, Lol Spence, Terry Spencer and Mike Turner.

I have met more briefly, or spoken on the telephone, with: Trevor Bailey, Gordon Barker, Donald Carr, Ken Cranston, Roger Goadby, Tom Graveney, Doug Insole, Ray Julian, Mike Roberts, Dennis Silk, Nigel Sisson, Brian Smith, Micky Stewart and Bob Wilson.

My publisher Stephen Chalke has provided me with contributions from the following: Michael Barton, Jack Birkenshaw, Tom Cartwright, Eric Hill, Rupert Webb and the late Maurice Hallam.

For help in putting me in touch with former pupils of Bromsgrove School, my thanks are due to Peter Fielden.

I am especially grateful for the help afforded me by Sylvia Michael, Leicestershire County Cricket Club archivist, and for access to MCC minutes my thanks are due to Adam Chadwick and Glenys Williams.

For free access to the product of his researches into Charles' early life, I am indebted to Davinder Sandhu.

Above all, I have had the pleasure of talking at length with Charles himself and with Barbara, his wife, and I remain grateful for their hospitality on my many visits to their Leicester home. I have also enjoyed talking with their sons Andrew and Tim. I have benefited immeasurably from having access to Charles' meticulously arranged scrap books, published articles, photographs and other papers.

I am grateful to Stephen Chalke for entrusting me with the task of writing this book and for his support and guidance as editor and publisher. I am also grateful to David Smith of Corsham for his meticulous and thoughtful proof-reading and to Susanna Kendall for her design of the jacket.

Most of the photographs in the book belong to Charles Palmer, though a few are from the Leicestershire County Cricket Club archives. Some – including the delightful colour photograph of Charles Palmer on the front flap – are reproduced by kind permission of Neville Chadwick. If inadvertently any photograph has been reproduced, the copyright of which belongs to another photographic source, they should contact Fairfield Books to rectify the matter.

I have referred freely to the following reference books:
Wisden Cricketers' Almanack
Playfair Cricket Annual
The Wisden Book of Obituaries (Macdonald Queen Anne Press, 1986)

Bailey, Thorn and Wynne-Thomas, *Who's Who of Cricketers*
       (Newnes Books, 1986)
Swanton, Plumptre and Woodcock, *Barclays Book of Cricket* (Collins, 1986)
Leicestershire County Cricket Club Annuals

I have also drawn material and occasionally quoted from:
David Rayvern Allen, *A Word from Arlott* (Pelham, 1983)
David Rayvern Allen, *Jim, The Life of EW Swanton* (Aurum, 2004)
Jack Bailey, *Conflicts in Cricket* (Kingswood Press, 1989)
Trevor Bailey, *Wickets, Catches and the Odd Run* (Willow Books, 1986)
Alex Bannister, *Cricket Cauldron* (Stanley Paul, 1954)
Henry Blofeld, *The Packer Affair* (Collins, 1978)
Don Bradman, *Farewell to Cricket* (Hodder & Stoughton, 1950)
Denis Compton, *The End of an Innings* (Oldbourne Book Company, 1958)
Dickie Dodds, *Hit Hard and Enjoy It* (The Cricketer, 1976)
Godfrey Evans, *Action in Cricket* (Hodder and Stoughton, 1956)
Tom Graveney, *Cricket Through The Covers* (Frederick Muller, 1958)
Brigadier M.A. Green, *Sporting Campaigner* (Stanley Paul, 1956)
Len Hutton with Alex Bannister, *Fifty Years in Cricket* (Hutchinson, 1984)
Jim Laker, *Spinning Round the World* (Frederick Muller, 1957)
Dennis Lambert, *The History of Leicestershire County Cricket Club*
       (Christopher Helm, 1992)
Michael Manley, *A History of West Indies Cricket* (Guild Publishing, 1988)
David Matthews, *On The Spot: A Biography of Derek Shackleton*
       (Blackberry Downs Books, 1998)
Peter Roebuck, *From Sammy to Jimmy* (Partridge Press, 1991)
David Sheppard, *Parson's Pitch* (Hodder & Stoughton, 1964)
EE Snow, *A History of Leicestershire Cricket* (Edgar Backus, 1949)
EW Swanton, *As I Said at the Time* (Collins Willow, 1983)
EW Swanton, *Sort of a Cricket Person* (Collins, 1972)
EW Swanton, *West Indian Adventure* (Museum Press 1954)
Clyde Walcott, *Island Cricketer* (Hodder & Stoughton, 1958)
Frank Worrell, *Cricket Punch* (Stanley Paul, 1959)

For much of the statistical information in the text, I have relied extensively on the CricketArchive website.

I have consulted and quoted from the magazine The Cricketer and from the following newspapers: Daily Express, Daily Herald, Daily Mail, Daily Telegraph, Manchester Guardian, News Chronicle, Observer, The Times, Birmingham Gazette, Birmingham Evening Mail, Birmingham Post, Leicester Evening Mail, Leicester Mercury, Wolverhampton Express and Star and Worcester News and Times.

Douglas Miller
July 2005

INDEX

(close family omitted)

Charles Palmer's cine films

When Charles Palmer toured **South Africa in 1948/49**, he shot several reels of film with a cine camera. More than fifty years later, he returned to these films. A 46-minute videotape was created, with footage both of the cricket itself and of the tour party travelling about South Africa, and Charles added his own commentary.

Copies of this South African video are for sale at **£14**, including postage.

Charles Palmer also took some film of his tour of **West Indies in 1953/54**, but inevitably his duties as tour manager prevented him from giving so much time to his filming. Nevertheless, there is now a 26-minute videotape from this tour, with footage that includes Tony Lock's quicker ball and the aftermath of the bottle-throwing in the Georgetown Test. Again Charles has provided a commentary.

Copies of this West Indian video are for sale at **£11**, including postage.

All proceeds from the sale of the videos are going to the family of Charles Palmer.

Orders should be sent to 1 Park Hill Avenue, Leicester LE2 8HQ and cheques made payable to **The MCC Tours**.

FAIRFIELD BOOKS

17 George's Road, Fairfield Park, Bath BA1 6EY · Tel: 01225-335813
The following books are available from Fairfield Books. Post free in the UK

Born To Bowl – The Life and Times of Don Shepherd

by Douglas Miller
The story of the much-loved Glamorgan cricketer.
This no-frills biography chronicles a bowler of wonderful skill and a man who exudes quality. I recommend it.
Christopher Martin-Jenkins, THE TIMES
Hardback, b&w illustrations, 224pp £15
ISBN: 0954488601

Runs in the Memory – County Cricket in the 1950s

by Stephen Chalke
illustrated by Ken Taylor
Twelve county cricket matches recalled by those who played in them.
Quite riveting. Right up my street – any romantic's street, in fact. Unquestionably the book of the year. Frank Keating, THE GUARDIAN
Paperback, b&w illustrations, 192pp £10
ISBN: 0953119653

One More Run

by Stephen Chalke,
with Bryan 'Bomber' Wells
The joyful reminiscences of Gloucestershire's Bomber Wells, woven around cricket at the Cheltenham Festival.
A blissful remembrance of a time when cricket and the world were different.
Michael Parkinson, DAILY TELEGRAPH
Paperback, b&w illustrations, 128pp £8
ISBN: 0953119629

Fragments of Idolatry – from 'Crusoe' to Kid Berg

by David Foot
Twelve sportsmen and writers admired by the award-winning author.
Sports writing on another plane.
Ian Wooldridge, DAILY MAIL
Hardback, b&w illustrations, 176pp £15
ISBN: 0953119637

The Appeal of the Championship – Sussex in the Summer of 1981

by John Barclay
foreword by Rt Rev David Sheppard
The story of Sussex's quest for their first championship, told by their captain.
Full of charm, wit and entertainment.
Tim Rice, DAILY TELEGRAPH
Hardback, b&w illustrations, 160pp £14
ISBN: 0953119661

Harold Gimblett – Tormented Genius of Cricket

by David Foot
foreword by the late John Arlott
The classic biography of the great Somerset batsman who took his own life.
A disturbing book. It stays with you, hauntingly, long after you've put it down.
David Frith, WISDEN CRICKET MONTHLY
Hardback, b&w illustrations, 176pp £15
ISBN: 095311967X

Guess My Story – The Life and Opinions of Keith Andrew

by Stephen Chalke
foreword by Micky Stewart
The story of the gifted and perceptive Northants and England wicket-keeper.
What he was and is, what he stands for and what he values, can be found in the pages of this splendid book. Robin Marlar, THE CRICKETER
Hardback, b&w illustrations, 192pp £15
ISBN: 0953119688

NOW OUT OF PRINT

No Coward Soul – The Remarkable Story of Bob Appleyard
by Stephen Chalke and Derek Hodgson

At the Heart of English Cricket – The Life and Memories of Geoffrey Howard
by Stephen Chalke

Caught in the Memory – County Cricket in the 1960s
by Stephen Chalke
